Guidelines for Landscape and Visual Impact Assessment

Second edition

Guidelines for Landscape and Visual Impact Assessment

Second edition

The Landscape Institute with the
Institute of Environmental
Management and Assessment

THE
LANDSCAPE
INSTITUTE

iema
Institute of Environmental
Management & Assessment

London and New York

First published 2002
by Spon Press
11 New Fetter Lane, London EC4P 4EE

Simultaneously published in the USA and Canada
by Spon Press
29 West 35th Street, New York, NY 10001

Spon Press is an imprint of the Taylor & Francis Group

Typeset in Stone Serif and Stone Sans by Bookcraft Ltd, Stroud, Gloucestershire
Printed and bound in The European Union by Mateu Cromo

British Library Cataloguing in Publication Data
A catalogue record for this book is available from the British Library

Library of Congress Cataloging in Publication Data
Guidelines for landscape and visual impact assessment/the Landscape Institute with the Institute of Environmental Management and Assessment – 2nd ed.
  p. cm.
  Includes bibliographical references
  1. Landscape assessment 2. Landscape protection 3. Environmental impact analysis
  I. Landscape Institute II. Institute of Environmental Management and Assessment
GF90 .G58 2001
712–dc21   2001049360

ISBN 0–415–23185–X

Contents

Foreword

When the Landscape Institute and the Institute of Environmental Assessment produced the first edition of these guidelines in 1995, they could have had no idea of how successful they would be – they have become the benchmark for landscape and visual assessment.

No Public Inquiry into planning matters seems complete without the guidelines being waved in the air.

That said, techniques and Government policy continue to develop and the guidelines need to keep abreast of developing legislation and new techniques. From a robust testing of the first edition, we now have the next stage in the ongoing evolution of landscape and visual assessment.

David Jarvis
President of the Landscape Institute

Preface

The good practice *Guidelines for Landscape and Visual Impact Assessment* (GLVIA) have been updated by the Landscape Institute, assisted by the Institute of Environmental Management and Assessment. They have been prepared by a Working Party and consultees comprising representatives from a wide range of interests, including professionals undertaking landscape and visual assessments, clients commissioning assessments, officers responsible for reviewing environmental statements and barristers who examine the results of assessments at Public Inquiries. Thanks must also be given to the sponsors: the Countryside Agency, Scottish Natural Heritage, the Environment Agency and National Grid for their help and support, and to the Planning Inspectorate for its useful guidance.

This second edition of the GLVIA is based on current best practice developed from the experience of Landscape Institute (LI) and Institute of Environmental Management and Assessment (IEMA) members over the last five years. It is, however, assumed that methodologies for landscape and visual impact assessment will continue to evolve in response to new approaches and different forms of development. In addition, in the rapidly changing conditions of development planning and environmental regulation, the guidelines can only reflect the conditions, terms and definitions at the time of publication. It is therefore expected that this document will continue to be periodically reviewed and updated in the light of evolving practice and legislation.

The Working Party members were:

Mary O'Conner	Bob Branson
Richard Burden	Gary Coulson
Jaquelin Fisher	Karl Fuller
Rebecca Hughes	Helen Kennedy
Martin Leay	Alan Moss
Conor Skehan	Jeff Stevenson
Ken Trew	Mark Turnbull
Sue Wilson	

The guidelines represent the consensus views of Working Party members, working on behalf of the Landscape Institute and the Institute of Environmental Management and Assessment, but not necessarily the views of their employers.

Susan R. Wilson
Chair of the GLVIA Working Group and Landscape Institute
Environment Committee

Summary

These guidelines are designed to encourage high standards for the scope and content of landscape and Visual Impact Assessments. Landscape and visual effects are independent but related issues; landscape effects are changes in the landscape, its character and quality, while visual effects relate to the appearance of these changes and the resulting effect on visual amenity. These guidelines aim to present general guidance on good practice in the preparation of landscape and visual impact assessments.

The statutory framework for Environmental Impact Assessment provides the basis for the methodology set out in the guidelines. However, it is also recognised that the Environmental Assessment process used in EIA may benefit other projects, for which an EIA is not formally required, in helping to achieve environmentally sensitive and sustainable development. Landscape and visual impact assessments can thus be an important part of the iterative process of development planning and design, through which the best environmental fit for development may be achieved. Within this context, the EIA process can help to achieve new developments that are sustainable and may also contribute to environmental enhancement.

An understanding of the nature of the proposed development is vital to landscape and visual impact assessments, including consideration of alternatives and all aspects that could affect the landscape and visual amenity throughout a project's life cycle. The baseline information for the assessments, obtained through comprehensive desk and field studies, should include description, classification and analysis of the landscape and visual resource. The assessment process identifies likely landscape and visual effects, establishes their magnitude and sensitivity of the receptor, and determines the significance of the effects. Mitigation measures – designed to avoid, reduce, remedy or offset negative or adverse effects – are identified, and their likely effectiveness also assessed.

EIA informs both decision makers and the public of the environmental effects of a development and presentation of the assessment requires careful consideration. Descriptions of the project and its likely effects should be supported by pertinent illustrative material. Consultation with deciion-making authorities, statutory bodies and the public is an important part of the process. Finally, following receipt of a planning consent for the development, monitoring should be carried out during implementation of the project and the establishment of the mitigation measures, in order to ensure these meet agreed performance standards.

Part 1

Introduction

Background

Environmental Impact Assessment (EIA), of which landscape and visual assessments are essential components, is an environmental management tool which has been in use on an international basis since 1970. It is a process by which the identification, prediction and evaluation of the key environmental effects of a development are undertaken and by which the information gathered is used to reduce likely negative effects during the design of the project and then to inform the decision-making process.

1.1

EIA became a statutory part of the planning process within the European Union through Council Directive 85/337/EEC [1]. In 1997, Directive 97/11/EC, which amends the 1985 Directive, extended the range of qualifying development to which the Directive applies and makes a number of changes to the way that EIA should be carried out [2]. The guidelines have been amended to accommodate these and related changes to the regulations. The terminology of the Directive has also been adopted in the guidelines; thus *impact* assessment refers to the process of environmental, landscape or visual impact assessment, while the changes resulting from the development that are assessed are referred to as the *effects*. It is noted, however, that the terms impact and effects are used synonymously in practice to refer to the changes brought about by development.

1.2

In the United Kingdom (UK), the majority of development tends to be dealt with under the Town and Country Planning Acts and related regulations. However, EIA is also a requirement for various types of development or activity falling within the ambit of other regulations, including forestation, land drainage improvement works, highways, pipelines, harbour and electricity works.

1.3

It is important to recognise that the guidelines do not exist in isolation and the reader's attention is drawn to other guidance that is relevant to landscape and visual assessments, in order to seek a common language and broader understanding of landscape issues. Of particular note is the Countryside Agency/Scottish Natural Heritage publication *Landscape Character Assessment: Guidance for England and Scotland* (forthcoming), which provides a basic guide to the approach and methods of landscape character assessment. In many cases, other reference documents also provide more comprehensive explanation and guidance on specific issues than could be accommodated in these guidelines.

1.4

Landscape and visual impact assessment is an evolving practice that continues developing to take account of new issues and assessment techniques. These include, among others, the continued importance of landscape character assessment and the greater emphasis on process and public participation, the development of systems for assessing environmental and 'quality of life' capital, and the increased use of Strategic Environmental Assessment. Landscape professionals

1.5

are accordingly advised to keep informed of any new guidance and techniques as they arise.

1.6 Since the publication of the first guidelines in 1995, there have been substantial developments and change within the landscape profession in the UK. In 1997, the Landscape Institute received a Royal Charter of Incorporation, and was thereby confirmed as the recognised professional body for all landscape matters. The holistic view of landscape professionals and scope of their interests, embodied in the charter, is of particular relevance and value in Environmental Impact Assessment.

1.7 Government policy has continued to embrace sustainable development, with further protection and enhancement of the environment as an integral part of planning for new development. Baseline landscape character assessments have also now been carried out for much of the UK.

1.8 Government guidance draws attention to the protection of landscape character and quality, placing an increasing pressure on local regulatory authorities to take these issues into account in all decision making that concerns landscapes. Planning authorities have also become more confident about exercising their power under the EIA regulations and there is greater public awareness of the effect of development on the landscape and higher public aspirations for its use and protection.

1.9 Landscape professionals play significant roles in the multidisciplinary teams of a substantial percentage of EIAs. Although the standard and content of environmental statements (ES) has been raised, through growing experience, there is also continuing concern that many could be improved. As a result, there continues to be a clear need for sound, reliable and widely-accepted advice on good practice for all aspects of EIA.

Aims of the guidelines

1.10 The principal aim of the guidelines is to encourage high standards for the scope and content of landscape and visual impact assessments, based on the collegiate opinion and practice of members of the Landscape Institute and the Institute of Environmental Management and Assessment. The guidelines also seek to establish certain principles that will help to achieve consistency, credibility and effectiveness in landscape and visual impact assessment, when carried out as part of an EIA.

1.11 The intent of the GLVIA is to present a general overview of a *non-specific* methodology for undertaking assessments of developments. It is the primary responsibility of landscape professionals carrying out assessments to first ensure that the approach and methodology adopted is appropriate for the particular development to be assessed. Secondly, they should ensure that, for each development proposed, the application of the method to the case in hand results in an assessment that is in accordance with the requirements of the current legal and planning framework.

Guidance is given here on some approaches and techniques, for aspects of the 1.12 assessment process, which have been found to be effective and useful in practice by landscape professionals. Case studies of projects are also included throughout the text to provide examples of current practice and clarification of points made. However, the guidelines are not intended as a prescriptive set of rules nor as an exhaustive manual of techniques.

Finally, the GLVIA aims to provide guidance for and meet the requirements of 1.13 landscape professionals involved in landscape and visual impact assessments. However, it is also recognised that they may be of some value to others with an interest in the EIA process, and to aid their understanding of landscape and visual assessments. These may include:

- developers and members of professional development project teams;

- those responsible for managing EIA and for ES review;

- planners and others within local government and the government agencies;

- academics and students of landscape design and EIA;

- politicians, amenity societies and the general public.

Scope of the guidelines

Part 1 provides the background and sets out the principal aims and scope of this 1.14 second edition of the guidelines.

Part 2 presents some common defining characteristics that underlie the approach 1.15 to landscape and visual impact assessments, which may also be applied to all forms and scales of development for which an EIA is not formally required. It outlines the role of landscape and visual impact assessments within the process of sound landscape planning, and provides a brief explanation of the terms that are used.

Part 3 addresses the statutory framework to the EIA process including a brief 1.16 consideration of the EC Directive, associated regulations and development planning in the context of the EIA process as a whole.

Part 4 considers the development proposals that may give rise to potential effects 1.17 and the need to describe alternative scheme options considered by the developer.

Part 5 addresses potential mitigation measures and techniques that may be 1.18 applied at all stages of the scheme development – to avoid, reduce, remedy or to offset negative effects.

1.19   *Part 6* describes the activities involved in the collection and collation of baseline studies and landscape character assessment.

1.20   *Part 7* addresses the identification of landscape and visual effects and the impact assessment process in detail.

1.21   *Part 8* sets out basic presentation techniques, which may be of use in the assessment process and in the production of the assessment report, contributions to an environmental statement and the non-technical summary.

1.22   *Part 9* deals with consultation, review and implementation. The role of consultation with both statutory agencies and the general public is explored. Advice is also given for the Regulatory Authorities who have an important role in screening and agreeing the scope and technical content of the assessment and in applying and monitoring landscape conditions following planning permission.

1.23   Finally, attention is also drawn to the expanded glossary of terms used in these guidelines, which includes detailed explanations current at the time of publication, and also to the information contained in the technical appendices.

Part 2

The nature of landscape and visual impact assessments

Introduction

Landscape encompasses the whole of our external environment, whether within villages, towns, cities or in the countryside. The nature and pattern of buildings, streets, open spaces and trees – and their interrelationships within the built environment – are equally important parts of our landscape heritage. 2.1

In both urban and rural contexts, the landscape is important because it is: 2.2

- an essential part of our natural resource base;

- a reservoir of archaeological and historical evidence;

- an environment for plants and animals (including humans);

- a resource that evokes sensual, cultural and spiritual responses and contributes to our urban and rural quality of life;

- a valuable recreation resource.

Landscapes are considerably more than just the visual perception of a combination of landform, vegetation cover and buildings – they embody the history, land use, human culture, wildlife and seasonal changes of an area. These elements combine to produce distinctive local character and continue to affect the way in which the landscape is experienced and valued. However, the landscape is also dynamic, continually evolving in response to natural or man-induced processes. 2.3

The assessment of landscape and visual impact has certain defining features that distinguish it from the methodologies used in the assessment of environmental impact in other topics. The sections below describe the basic principles that underlie the process and provide an introduction to the detailed parts of this book that deal with methodology and techniques. 2.4

Landscape and visual impact assessments may also be different from other specialist studies because they are generally undertaken by professionals who are also involved in the design of the landscape and the preparation of subsequent management proposals. This can allow the assessment to proceed as an integral part of the overall scheme design, rather than as a discreet study carried out once the proposals have been finalised. 2.5

EIA proceeds on several fronts at once. Site surveys and preliminary assessments can be carried out concurrently with the development of the initial project proposal, and steps can be reiterated in the process to refine the design proposal. Certain potential effects can also be identified at an early stage from the knowledge gained from the site surveys, and these can be addressed during the development of the scheme. Other effects may become apparent as the assessment progresses. 2.6

A rural landscape showing different aspects of the landscape resource: land use and management, ecological features, buildings and landforms

Landscape and visual effects are two of the issues addressed as part of an Environmental Impact Assessment

2.7   The role of EIA in the development process is recognised as an integral part of the planning and decision-making process. Its strength lies in its potential for analysing the associated environmental issues and for improving the siting, layout and design of a particular scheme. The assessments of landscape and visual effects are an essential part of this process. Environmental assessment can thus be appropriate for all forms and scales of development, not just for those for which an EIA is mandatory.

2.8   For each key topic identified in the EC Directive, it is important that the methodology used for the assessment is clearly set out. This will normally include a baseline survey, identification of effects and sensitive receptors, description and quantification of the changes to the baseline, and the evaluation of predicted effects, together with criteria used and the measures proposed to avoid, reduce, remedy or offset negative effects. The reader of the assessment – whether planning authority, member of the public, planning inspector or barrister at a Public Inquiry – must be able to recognise that a rigorous process has been applied.

2.9   The fundamental components of EIA, which should be followed in landscape and visual impact assessments, are set out in Part 3.

A townscape in Hampshire, illustrating the urban nature of the landscape. The interrelationship between buildings and open spaces, plants and other elements combine to create the urban landscape

Landscape and visual impact assessments are different to most studies carried out as part of an EIA because it is not possible to quantify all aspects

For some topics, such as water or air quality, it is possible to use measurable, technical international or national guidelines or legislative standards, against which potential effects can be assessed. The assessment of likely effects on a landscape resource and on visual amenity is more complex, since it is determined through a combination of quantitative and qualitative evaluations. 2.10

Landscape impact assessment, in common with any assessment of environmental effects, includes a combination of objective and subjective judgements, and it is therefore important that a structured and consistent approach is used. It is necessary to differentiate between judgements that involve a degree of subjective opinion (as in the assessment of landscape value) from those that are normally more objective and quantifiable (as in the determination of magnitude of change). (See Figure 2.1.) 2.11

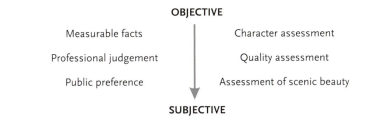

Figure 2.1   Components of EIA

Source: N.P. Brown (Principal Landscape Conservation Officer, Warwickshire County Council), *Landscape Evaluation Guidelines and their use for Land Use Planning*, February 1996.

2.12 Judgement should always be based on training and experience and be supported by clear evidence and reasoned argument. Accordingly, it is recommended that suitably qualified and experienced landscape professionals carry out landscape and visual impact assessments.

Landscape and visual effects are assessed separately

2.13 Landscape and visual assessments are separate, although linked, procedures. The landscape baseline, its analysis and the assessment of landscape effects all contribute to the baseline for visual assessment studies. The assessment of the potential effect on the landscape is carried out as an effect on an environmental resource, i.e. the landscape. Visual effects are assessed as one of the interrelated effects on population [2, 3].

2.14 Landscape effects derive from changes in the physical landscape, which may give rise to changes in its character and how this is experienced. This may in turn affect the perceived value ascribed to the landscape. The description and analysis of effects on a landscape resource relies on the adoption of certain basic princi-ples about the positive (or beneficial) and negative (or adverse) effects of change in the landscape. Due to the inherently dynamic nature of the landscape, change arising from a development may not necessarily be significant.

2.15 Visual effects relate to the changes that arise in the composition of available views as a result of changes to the landscape, to people's responses to the changes, and to the overall effects with respect to visual amenity.

Assessment of effects on the landscape resource considers the different aspects of landscape

2.16 In order to reach an understanding of the effects of development on a landscape resource, it is necessary to consider the different aspects of the landscape, as follows:

- **Elements** The individual elements that make up the landscape, including prominent or eye-catching features such as hills, valleys, woods, trees and hedges, ponds, buildings and roads. They are generally quantifiable and can be easily described.

- **Characteristics** Elements or combinations of elements that make a particular contribution to the character of an area, including experiential characteristics such as tranquillity and wildness.

- **Character** The distinct and recognisable pattern of elements that occurs consistently in a particular type of landscape, and how this is perceived by people. It reflects particular combinations of geology, landform, soils, vege-tation, land use and human settlement. It creates the particular sense of place of different areas of the landscape. Character is identified through the process of characterisation, which classifies, maps and describes areas of similar character.

The process of landscape character assessment can increase appreciation of what 2.17   **13**
makes the landscape distinctive and what is important about an area, and can
also improve the understanding of change both in urban areas and the countryside. It thereby contributes to our understanding of the form and pattern of the
landscape at a range of scales (national, regional or district). However, to undertake a project-based landscape impact assessment as part of an EIA, it will be
necessary to undertake more detailed localised studies.

Environmental impact assessment and landscape design are iterative processes

An iterative design approach enables the site planning and detailed design of a 2.18
development project to be informed by and respond to the ongoing Environmental Impact Assessment, as the environmental constraints and opportunities are taken into consideration at each stage of decision making. Experience
indicates that this approach can result in more successful and cost-effective
developments, and can reduce the time required to complete the assessment.
The iterative approach is appropriate to any new development of whatever
scale or type, whether or not it requires a full EIA. The iterative approach is
illustrated in Figure 2.2.

Landscape and visual impact assessments are important parts of the iterative 2.19
design process because they can help to avoid or minimise potential negative
effects of the development and, where appropriate, can also help in seeking
opportunities for landscape enhancement. During site selection and the initial
design of the layout for the development, the landscape architect may produce:

- land use/landscape strategies to evaluate and address constraints, taking
  advantage of environmental opportunities for each of the options available;

- comparative appraisals of alternative options, to identify those with least
  overall adverse environmental effect on the landscape and visual amenity.

Once the preferred development option has been selected, the landscape profes- 2.20
sional works with the design team to:

- identify and develop measures to further reduce residual adverse environmental impacts, taking into account the landscape management
  implications;

- indicate how the landscape strategy will work in practice, on completion of
  the development and throughout the lifetime of the project;

- prepare landscape and visual impact assessments to address in detail the
  residual landscape and visual effects of the proposed development.

Initial project planning	Identify site requirements; predict likely impacts of the proposed development for consideration in site selection.
Screening	Ascertain if EIA required.
Scoping	Establish content (scope) of the EIA (if required).
Alternative sites (If appropriate)	Carry out comparative site appraisals for alternative sites, e.g. desk studies of planning policy; site infrastructure needs; access; baseline environmental data including landscape and visual site appraisal to test the relative suitability of alternative sites for the development.
	Preliminary consultations with regulatory authority, statutory consultees and others (e.g. the public).
Preferred solution	Collate baseline environmental data and carry out technical studies, including baseline landscape and visual resources and identification of potential receptors.
	Consult statutory and other consultees.
Conceptual design	Assess the implications of the design against baseline information.
	Identify likely positive/negative effects to ensure 'optimum environmental fit'.
	Consider design options.
Modify design to avoid effects	Reassess potential effects.
	Identify potential mitigation measures to reduce negative effects.
Refine design to incorporate measures to reduce adverse effects	If appropriate, reassess potential negative effects.
	Identify further mitigation measures to remedy outstanding negative effects;
	Consultations with regulatory authority.
Final design incorporating further remediation measures if appropriate	Review the assessment of effects against the final scheme parameters.
	Consider proposals to compensate for residual/ unavoidable effects.
	Complete Environmental Statement (if an EIA is required).
Planning Application	Review of ES by regulatory/competent authority and consultees.
	Evaluation of ES by regulatory authority.
Decision	
Implementation and monitoring	

Figure 2.2 The iterative design approach

In some instances, a separate Environmental Assessment team, independent of the design team, may be appointed to explicitly demonstrate that the assessment is objective and without bias, particularly with respect to the evaluation of effects and the likely success of any proposed mitigation measures. 2.21

The description of the alternatives that have been considered by a developer is now a formal requirement of the EIA process. The iterative process can be helpful in providing evidence that alternative sites and/or designs have been assessed, and it is therefore important to record how the scheme has developed throughout the life of the project. This will demonstrate how landscape and visual effects have been taken into account and why some options have been rejected. 2.22

The baseline study includes the identification of those landscape elements, and characteristics that are valued and the people by whom they are valued

Changes in the landscape can have a direct and immediately apparent effect upon people's surroundings. It is therefore necessary to identify the landscape components that are valued by the community or society as a whole, why and how they are valued and, where possible, the people to whom they are valuable – that is 'what matters and why'. 2.23

The determination of landscape value can be based on particular characteristics that contribute to a 'sense of place' or influence the way in which a landscape is experienced, and on special interests such as cultural and literary associations, nature conservation or heritage interests. Landscape value may also incorporate a description of the condition of the landscape elements and features, and the way that they contribute to its character. 2.24

The particular characteristics of the landscape may be used to define policy areas that are deemed to reflect the value of the landscape to society as a whole. At a national scale (for example, the National Parks), the broad-brush nature of these designations and their boundaries will require more detailed studies at a site-specific scale, to establish what is important about the landscape affected by a development, and to whom it is important. 2.25

Landscapes may also have value because of the function they perform regardless of the character of the landscape. Thus urban fringe landscapes may be of poor condition with no special interest, but may nevertheless be highly valued locally because they are accessible to people and may represent a scarce landscape resource in that particular area. 2.26

The capacity of a particular landscape to accommodate change varies with the type of development proposed

2.27   The sensitivity of the landscape to change is reflected in the degree to which a landscape is able to accommodate change (due to a particular development or land use change) without adverse effects on its character [4]. This may be influenced by the extent of existing or new landform and/or existing vegetation or new planting. These and other factors determine the visibility of the proposed development and therefore influence the extent of its effect on the perceived character and visual amenity of the surrounding landscape.

2.28   Landscapes vary in their capacity to accommodate different forms of development. Sensitivity is thus not absolute but is likely to vary according to the existing landscape, the nature of the proposed development and the type of change being considered. Sensitivity is not therefore part of the landscape baseline, but is considered during the assessment of effects.

2.29   The capacity of the landscape to accommodate development is quite different from the importance or value of the landscape. These issues are therefore dealt with separately.

The significance of the effects may be influenced by, but not determined by, planning policies and designation.

2.30   In EIA, it is necessary to make a broad assessment of the likelihood of significant effects at the screening and scoping stages, based on the nature, size or location of the proposed development and the scale of its likely environmental effects. For this initial stage of assessment, it is usually assumed that formally designated landscapes are more likely to be sensitive to change than other areas. Similarly, some forms of development are also considered more likely to give rise to significant effects if, for example, they include particular operations or processes, or are of a particularly large scale.

2.31   Once the likely main or significant effects have been identified, the purpose of the EIA is to describe these effects and the proposals for their mitigation. EIAs deal with a specific set of proposals for a specific site (or sites) and it is important to avoid generalisations in the assessment process itself. A case-by-case approach is therefore recommended, and for each situation the likely effect on the landscape elements, characteristics and overall character is assessed and its significance judged on the basis of the nature and magnitude of effect and the sensitivity (including value or importance) of those elements, characteristics and character.

2.32   Landscape designation (as a reflection of value to society) is thus only one of a number of criteria that are considered in identifying the relative 'sensitivity' of the landscape to a proposed development. It should not be used in isolation.

The presentation and reasoning behind professional judgements included in the   2.33
assessment of landscape and visual effects need to be clear for a number of
reasons:

- there may be complex interrelationships with other topics, for example,
  nature conservation, cultural heritage and land use;

- they are not easily measured and thus rely on precise language;

- assessment includes some subjective judgements;

- landscape and visual effects can attract emotive public responses for
  example, from visitors or residents, which should be distinguished from
  the professional's judgements.

The systematic and detailed approach to landscape and visual impact assessment   2.34
set out in these guidelines may contrast with alternative responses to a development that may be presented by the public or objectors during consultations.
Emotional statements do not assist in making balanced and reasoned decisions.
Nevertheless, it is important that such alternative views, where available, are
acknowledged in the preparation of the assessment, since they represent the
stakeholders' views of the effects of the development.

General principles of good practice

General principles for good practice in landscape and visual impact assessment   2.35
include:

- **clearly describe the methodology** and the specific techniques that
  have been used, so that the procedure is replicable and the results can be
  clearly understood by a lay person;

- **use clearly-defined and agreed terminology**, particularly when
  defining the sensitivity of landscape and visual resources, the magnitude of
  predicted effects and in determining their significance;

- **avoid generalisations** about designated landscapes and their ability to
  accommodate change;

- **be as impartial as possible**, and state the basis upon which each judgement is made;

- **draw upon the advice and opinions of others**, for example, in relation to special interests or values such as cultural and historic influences,
  ecology and the built environment;

- **carry out consultations** to identify, where possible, the value placed on a landscape and the effects resulting from a potential development by the local community and others;

- **organise and structure the assessment** to focus upon the key issues of relevance to decision making;

- **openly acknowledge any deficiencies** or limitations of data, techniques or resources that may have constrained the assessment;

- **consider the 'worst-case situation'**, where appropriate, in relation to seasonal or unknown effects or aspects of the proposal that are not fully developed.

Part 3

Background to the assessment

The legislative framework for EIA

This section provides a brief introduction to the legislative framework for landscape and visual impact assessments carried out as part of an EIA which in turn forms part of the system of development control for development projects within the EC. It is important to emphasise that EIA is a process that continues to evolve and as our understanding of our environment increases, so legislation evolves with it.

3.1

Good practice requires that the landscape professional, carrying out landscape and visual impact assessments as part of an EIA, should be aware that:

3.2

- the EIA process is applied by different regulations and guidance in different parts of the European Union (and United Kingdom) with respect to different forms of development and/or activity;

- its implementation through statute and regulation also continues to develop as regulations are introduced, amended and – from time to time – replaced.

EC Directive

The current statutory framework for an Environmental Impact Assessment and Environmental Statement within the European Union is Council Directive 97/1/EC. This is implemented in England and Wales by the Town and Country Planning (England and Wales) (Environmental Impact Assessment) Regulations 1999, and in Scotland by the Environmental Impact Assessment (Scotland) Regulations 1999. Additional guidance on interpretation of the Directive and regulations or equivalent for each country is normally provided by Government departments (see Appendix 1).

3.3

The Directive sets out a procedure for EIA that must be followed for certain types of project before they can be given 'development consent'. EIA is a means of systematically drawing together an assessment of a project's likely significant environmental effects. This helps to ensure that the importance of the predicted effects and the scope for reducing them are properly understood by the public and the relevant 'competent authority' before it makes its decision (see Appendix 2).

3.4

In essence, EIA (and as part of it the assessment of landscape and visual effects) considers information concerning:

3.5

- the attributes of the receiving environment;

- the nature of the development;

- the likely significant effects arising;

- measures to avoid, reduce, remedy and if possible offset any significant adverse effects on the environment;

- the main alternatives (if any) studied and the reasons for the scheme selected;

- the presentation of the above in an Environmental Statement (ES) and, in a simplified form, in a non-technical summary (NTS).

National regulations

3.6 Further guidance on the information to be included within an ES is given in the relevant regulations. However, neither the EC Directive nor the regulations prescribe any particular methodology to be used in carrying out the assessment.

3.7 The Directive also sets out the basic requirements. In their application of the Directive or in supplementary guidance, member states may – and generally do – go beyond the requirements of the Directive. An example from the regulations for England and Wales, which also reflects those for Scotland, is indicated in Box 3.1.

3.8 While the Directive is the starting point for a professional understanding of the legislative process, the regulations and associated advice or circulars vary in different parts of the United Kingdom and between member states, although they may follow a similar pattern. It is therefore good practice that landscape professionals not only familiarise themselves with the range of regulations, but also the individual requirements appropriate to each location.

Terminology

3.9 The legislative framework provides the backbone for an Environmental Statement. As the content of an ES should stand up to formal rigorous inspection, it is vital that the utmost care is taken in the use of terminology. Where terms used in the legislation are used in an Environmental Statement, they must be used in the same context. The Environmental Statement should contain a clear and unambiguous definition of such terms, which are in turn used in a consistent manner throughout.

The EIA process

3.10 A common assessment process for EIA is now emerging and the main steps in the process of landscape and visual assessment closely mirror the sequence of events that characterise the formal EIA process as a whole (see Appendix 3 and Figure 3.1). This section provides an overview of the process, which is summarised in Figure 3.1 and the flowchart in Figure 3.2.

Box 3.1   Extract from the EIA Regulations

The assessment of landscape and visual effects arises within the EIA process essentially through Article 3 of the 1997 Directive, which states

> The environmental impact assessment shall identify, describe and assess in an appropriate manner, in the light of each individual case and in accordance with Articles 4 to 11, the direct and indirect effects of a project on the following factors
>
> - **human beings**, fauna and flora;
> - soil, water, air, climate and **the landscape**;
> - material assets and the cultural heritage;
> - **the interaction between the factors** mentioned in the first, second and third indents.

In England and Wales, the requirements of the Directive are interpreted in Schedule 4 Part 1 (3) of the 1999 Regulations as

> A description of the aspects of the environment likely to be significantly affected by the development, including, in particular, **population**, fauna, flora, soil, water, air, climatic factors, material assets, including the architectural and archaeological heritage, **landscape** and the **inter-relationship between the above factors**.

While Schedule 4 Part I (4) also requires

> A description of the likely significant effects of the development on the environment, which should cover the direct effects and any indirect, secondary, cumulative, short, medium and long-term, permanent and temporary, positive and negative effects of the development resulting from
>
> – the existence of the development;
> – the use of natural resources;
> – the emission of pollutants, the creation of nuisances and the elimination of waste, and the description by the applicant of the forecasting methods used to assess the effects on the environment.

together with Schedule 4 Part I (5), which requires

> A description of the measures envisaged to prevent, reduce and where possible offset any significant adverse effects on the environment [2, 3].

Screening	Determines the need for an EIA.
Scoping	Identifies the scope and content of the EIA.
Project description	Provides a formal description of the development for the purpose of assessment including alternatives.
Baseline studies	Describes, classifies and evaluates the existing landscape and visual resource.
Assessment	The systematic identification of potential effects, prediction of their magnitude, and assessment of their significance.
Mitigation	Measures designed to avoid, reduce or offset negative effects of the development proposals.
Presentation of findings	These require a clear structure, plain language and good illustrative material.
Monitoring	Monitors the effects on sensitive elements of the construction and operation of the development to identify/prevent negative effects.

Figure 3.1   Elements in the EIA process

3.11   Screening is the crucial first step of an EIA. It is the formal process through which the decision on the need for an EIA is taken or confirmed by the 'competent authority', usually the local regulatory authority. This decision is based on the nature, location and size of the proposed development and a broad assessment of the likelihood and scale of the main or significant effects. The criteria for significance are usually defined in terms of the scale of the proposals, the sensitivity of the location and the nature of the development. An EIA may still be required even if there are no likely significant landscape or visual effects. An applicant may formally request a screening opinion from the local planning authority. The applicant's request would normally include basic information about the proposed development such as:

- a plan indicating the location of the proposed development;

- a brief description of the nature and purpose of the proposal;

- an indication of its possible main environmental effects;

- other information or representations as the applicant may wish to provide or make, such as a broad indication of the potential scale of the likely effects.

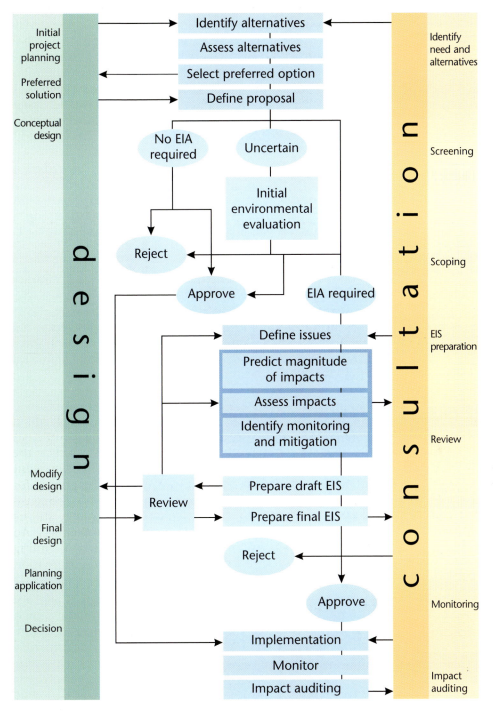

Figure 3.2 The EIA process

3.12 At this stage, landscape designations may be used as an indicator of the potential sensitivity of the landscape and likelihood of significant negative effects. The landscape professional may be called upon to provide a professional, albeit informal, opinion as to the potential sensitivity of the landscape or visual effects of a scheme. In making any judgements and providing such advice and opinion, the landscape professional should adopt a structured and systematic approach from the outset and record all actions undertaken, information gathered, issues taken into consideration, assumptions made and opinions offered, together with reasoned justification.

3.13 Scoping comprises the second stage in the EIA process and is the procedure of examining key topics and identifying areas of likely significant effects. The objective of scoping is to ensure that all relevant issues are addressed in the EIA. It is one of the most critical activities in the whole process; if it is wrong or incomplete, it can undermine the validity of the ES. It should not however be used to pre-judge the effect of a development at this early stage.

3.14 Scoping entails a desk study, site and scheme familiarisation and informal consultations with the 'competent authority' and the main consultees. Available national guidance on scoping should also be consulted. A request may also be made to the regulatory authority for a formal scoping opinion concerning the information to be supplied in the ES. This can help to ascertain the authority's opinion on what the main or significant effects are likely to be and to define the content or scope of the ES.

3.15 The landscape professional may seek agreement with the regulatory authority on the study area for the landscape and visual impact assessments, the potentially sensitive receptors and important or sensitive viewpoints.

3.16 An ES is not necessarily rendered invalid if it does not cover all the matters specified in the scoping opinion or directive, or because an applicant fails to provide further information when required to do so. However, if it is deemed that the applicant has failed to provide sufficient information on the environmental effects to enable the regulatory authority to make an informed decision, the planning application is likely to be refused.

3.17 If produced, a scoping document can set out the range of possible issues, explaining why each will or will not be evaluated in the assessment. It may also include brief details on methods, assessment techniques and the presentation of information to be included in the final ES. Although not mandatory, a scoping document can be helpful and may be prepared as a free-standing document or incorporated in the ES.

Methodology

The methodology for the landscape and visual assessments may be agreed with   3.18
the regulatory authority at the scoping stage. However, it must be recognised
that the methodology will need to be sufficiently flexible to allow modification,
as appropriate, in response to information collected during the baseline studies.

The methodology should be appropriate for the nature, location and scale of the   3.19
project and the potential sensitivity of the site, as established through screening
and scoping. For simple schemes, a relatively brief overall assessment of the
effects on the landscape and visual amenity may be sufficient; while large
complex schemes may require separate detailed assessments of each component
of the project in addition to an assessment of the overall effects of the
development.

National designation may be an indication of the potential for significant   3.20
effects. Accordingly, sites within or adjacent to nationally designated landscapes
require detailed and rigorous assessments that are appropriate to the status of the
landscape. Particular attention should be given to the special attributes and characteristics that justified the original designation, together with the policy objectives of the designation. The assessment of visual effects should also consider the
potential effects on views of as well as from the designated landscape from
important or valued viewpoints.

The likely means and extent of consultations may also be identified at this stage   3.21
and if appropriate discussed or agreed with the regulatory authority.

Planning policy context

Landscape and visual impact assessments are invariably carried out in order to   3.22
comply with the requirements of the development planning process. Landscape
professionals should be aware of the planning framework and context to the
proposed development that is being assessed, as this can be of benefit in helping
to identify and establish the issues which need to be considered in scoping the
EIA, particularly in relation to designations and policy objectives.

The EC Directive and EIA Regulations (England and Wales) make no reference to   3.23
supplying policy-relevant information within the EIA, although within England
and Wales Government guidance suggests that such information should be
included in the ES [5]. An analysis of relevant plans and policies, including the
degree of compliance or conflict of the development with the policies and other
relevant issues, is helpful in order to demonstrate how these policy guidelines have
been taken into account in developing the project and compiling the ES. It should
also provide a picture of the decision-making context in which the environmental

effects will be evaluated. In order to obtain benefit from this process, it is important to consider the planning context for the development at an early stage of site planning/design and assessment.

3.24 Where policy-relevant information is not provided as a separate section in the ES, the relevant planning policy information should be included in the report of the landscape and visual impact assessments.

3.25 The principal planning reference for determining an application is the development plan. This may be a combination of a strategic structure plan and local plan or a unitary development plan supported by supplementary planning guidance documents. It is particularly important because it allocates land uses and defines landscape policy and designation. In addition, there is generally a wide range of planning advice from Government, environmental agencies and other interest groups, which should also be considered where relevant (see Appendix 1 for further information).

Special interests

3.26 It is important for landscape assessments to consider the ecological, historical or cultural associations that contribute to the character and importance of a landscape. Habitats and wildlife have a visible effect on the appearance and also the appreciation and value of landscape, and planning policies for nature conservation and landscape are generally linked through a common approach to land use. Historic associations are often more intangible. However, there are also numerous interrelationships between landscape and cultural heritage and it is important that these links are not overlooked.

3.27 Historic landscapes can include gardens, battlefields and the statutory settings of listed buildings and ancient monuments. It may sometimes be unclear where priorities lie when non-statutory designations exist, or even which discipline is best-placed to assess them. Sometimes their cultural heritage value can run counter to any landscape value (as may be the case for some derelict industrial sites), with the possibility that assessments of landscape settings of historic sites by archaeologists and landscape architects could vary, due to the different focus of study and objectives. Such problems can be avoided by establishing a close liaison between landscape and cultural heritage specialists in the preparation of the EIA, and by each party focusing on their own planning policy context. This will also be of assistance in decision making, as it will enable information in the ES to be directly related to the relevant policy requirements [6].

3.28 Proposals for mitigating significant negative or adverse landscape effects can themselves have the potential to adversely affect cultural heritage sites and influence or change the nature conservation value or potential of an area. Any such potential problems should be reduced or avoided by close liaison between the professionals involved at all stages of the assessment and design process.

Sustainable development

The concept of sustainable development aims to conserve and enhance our envi-   3.29
ronment for the benefit of present and future generations through development
that meets the needs of the present without compromising the ability of future
generations to meet their own [7]. This does not mean that the landscape should
not change at all. This objective would be impossible to achieve, even if it were
desirable, as landscape change is inevitable. The land is intrinsically a living
resource and, in most developed countries, it is almost exclusively managed by
human intervention in natural processes. Changes in land management and the
effect of other developments in the area will alter its appearance and character.
Similarly townscapes evolve over time as buildings are replaced or added and
land use changes.

Box 3.2   Sustainability reference

The British Government has made 'Sustainable development' the
cornerstone of both its rural and planning policies. This is interpreted as
meaning that the countryside should be managed in ways that meet
current needs without compromising the ability of future generations to
meet their own needs.

The guidance goes on to state that development should respect and, where
possible, enhance the environment.

(See Appendix 1 and Planning Policy Guidance (PPG) 1)

Three principles from the Rio Earth Summit declaration (1992) are of particular   3.30
relevance to landscape and visual assessments:

- the promotion of environmental protection as an integral part of the development process, in order to achieve sustainable development;

- the participation at the relevant level of all concerned citizens in handling
  environmental issues with appropriate access to information;

- the need for Environmental Impact Assessment on developments that are
  likely to have adverse effects on the environment.

Since 1995, the planning context for landscape assessment has changed. The   3.31
guidance on sustainability gives greater attention to the value of all landscapes
(rather than just designated ones), and the need to accommodate change while
maintaining and, where possible, enhancing the quality of the environment for
local people and visitors. New development is also required to respect the environment in its location, scale and design.

3.32 The implications of sustainable development for the assessment of landscape and visual effects are considerable. It is accepted that development may create effects not just for the site itself and its immediate environs, but also for other areas. Thus the choice of construction materials for the construction of a new road, for example, may result in significant associated landscape and visual effects from quarrying, whereas the re-use of construction waste may actually help to avoid adverse landscape effects elsewhere as a result of its disposal.

3.33 EIA creates opportunities to contribute to sustainable development by seeking opportunities to 'conserve and enhance' landscape character and visual resources. Loss of landscape or visual resources due to development may be offset through landscape enhancement and additional measures, which genuinely compensate for any elements or particular features lost or damaged. These issues are considered in more detail in the section on mitigation in Part 5.

Strategic Environmental Impact Assessment

3.34 It is widely recognised that project-level EIA alone cannot lead to comprehensive environmental protection or sustainable development. The nature of assessing the impacts of individual proposals is a reactive approach that cannot fully address the cumulative effects that may arise from several projects. These may be avoided with a more proactive approach, which could predict or anticipate such effects. In recognition of such problems, the process of Strategic Environmental Assessment (SEA) was developed to address the environmental effects of proposed policies, plans or programmes. SEA is a process that evaluates the likely significant environmental consequences of a policy, plan or programme.

3.35 SEA is also one of the tools by which sustainable development and use of resources can be most effectively achieved. Simple steps toward sustainability such as efficient energy use, multi-modal transport design and specific land-use policies can be appraised and restructured through SEA to ensure that policies, plans and programmes are sustainable and hence that the projects which fall under these will be equally sustainable.

3.36 At an early stage of assessment, many SEAs rely on landscape designations as indicative of landscape importance and possible sensitivity. However, a more fundamental review that considers the contribution of landscape elements or features, characteristics and values as indicators of landscape sensitivity may be more appropriate for regional and district planning policy purposes, drawing on available character assessment information (see Appendix 4 for further information on Strategic Environmental Assessment).

Part 4

Description of the proposed development

Introduction

An assessment of landscape and visual effects is based on information concerning the attributes of the receiving environment and the location, scale and nature of the development.

4.1

Information about the development of relevance to the assessment needs to be assembled, kept under review during the planning and design stages, updated where appropriate and then 'fixed' to enable the assessment to be finalised, including:

4.2

- description of the development;

- consideration of alternatives;

- knowledge of the stages in the project's life cycle, extending from commencement of construction to restoration;

- the measures proposed to avoid, reduce and, if possible, offset any significant adverse effects on the environment. These are addressed in Part 5.

A general description of the siting, layout and characteristics of the proposed development is a formal planning requirement. A clear, concise but comprehensive description can also make an important contribution to the credibility and effectiveness of the EIA study.

4.3

The point at which the design is finalised for the purposes of assessment and preparation of the planning application must also be agreed, to permit assessment to proceed upon firm assumptions, forming the factual basis for impact identification and prediction. It is essential that the description of the development on which the impact assessment of the scheme is carried out is sufficiently detailed, to ensure the effects of the proposed development can be clearly identified. The level of detail provided will vary from project to project, but the minimum information usually required for an outline application will be insufficient for an EIA.

4.4

Consideration of alternatives

Where alternative development proposals have been considered by the developer, it is a requirement of the EIA regulations to provide an outline description of the main alternatives considered and an indication of the main reasons for the final development choice, taking into account the environmental effects. This may be particularly relevant for sensitive locations. Increasingly, consideration of alternative approaches to the development is seen to be good development practice and is encouraged as a means of achieving potentially more sustainable development. For some projects, such as those undertaken by the Highways Agency, the 'do nothing scenario' – against which the development will be compared – may be presented as an alternative.

4.5

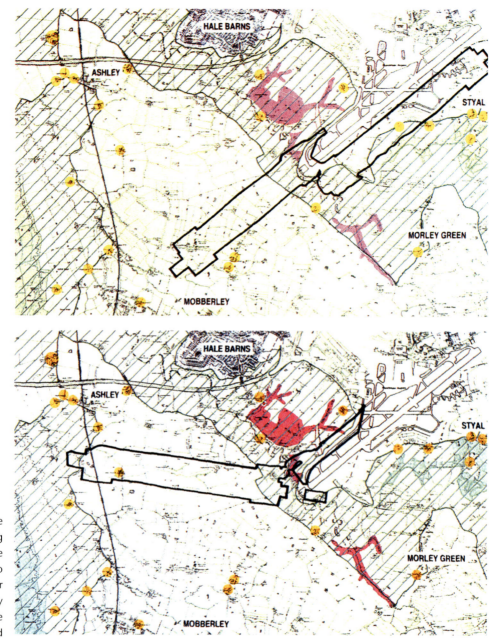

In this example
illustrating
alternative
layouts, two
options for
runway
alignments have
been assessed

4.6   The landscape professional may be required to advise on alternative solutions
that could include:

- alternative locations or sites that are suitable and available;

- different approaches in terms of scheme design, or the size/scale/orientation of the proposed development;

- alternative site layouts, access and servicing arrangements.

An important benefit of exploring alternatives is that they may offer significant opportunities for mitigating potentially negative (adverse) effects by avoidance of such effects or through the redesign of features that would otherwise give rise to negative effects. For example, if there are serious landscape constraints associated with a particular site, avoidance of effects through the selection of an alternative location is likely to be a preferred solution.

Depending on the type of study that is being carried out and the stage reached in 4.8 the assessment process, more than one project alternative may be taken forward for comparative assessment, with a detailed project description required for each alternative. The most common examples occur in the development of transport infrastructure, where route option appraisals for a number of alternative routes are frequently undertaken before a decision is made on the preferred route. Once the preferred route is selected, a more detailed assessment is then carried out. Many other types of project could benefit from a similar approach.

Stages in the project life cycle

It is recognised that project characteristics, and hence sources of effects, will vary 4.9 through time. The construction, operation, decommissioning and restoration phases of a development are characterised by quite different physical elements and activities. The duration of the effect is also a material consideration, since a lesser effect may be less tolerable if it continues for a significant period. A separate, self-contained description of the development at each stage in the life cycle greatly assists the prediction of landscape and visual effects.

For the **construction stage** of the project, the relevant information may 4.10 include:

- site access and haul routes, including traffic movements (which often differ from permanent access proposals);

- cut, fill, borrow and disposal areas;

- materials origins;

- materials stockpiles;

- staging areas;

- construction equipment and plant;

- utilities, including water, drainage, power and lighting;

- temporary parking and on-site accommodation and working areas;

- temporary screening measures;

- protection of existing features;

- lighting of the works.

4.11 During the **operational stage**, the matters likely to be most relevant to the landscape and visual impact assessments include:

- access;
- infrastructure;
- buildings and other structures;
- delivery, loading and unloading areas;
- outdoor activities;
- materials storage;
- land management operations and objectives;
- utilities;
- lighting of roads and buildings;
- car parking;
- vehicle lights and movement (and the effect of noise on landscape character);
- landform, structure planting and hard landscape features;
- entrances, signs and boundary treatments;
- the programme and details, including duration of any proposed phasing of the operations;
- areas of possible future development.

4.12 Decommissioning and restoration may also give rise to effects to be addressed, including:

- access;
- after-use potential;
- residual buildings and structures;
- disposal or recycling of wastes and residues;
- restoration activities, including movement of materials and construction plant around the site.

Information requirements

4.13 For each stage in the project life cycle, similar types of qualitative and quantitative data are required to assist in assessments of landscape and visual effects, including:

- form (including shape, bulk, pattern, edges, orientation, complexity and symmetry);

- materials (including texture, colour, shade, reflectivity, opacity);

- design (including layout, scale, style, distinctiveness);

- programme and duration of key site activities;

- site areas under different uses;

- physical dimensions of major construction plant, buildings and structures;

- volumes of material;

- numbers of scheme components such as houses and parking spaces;

- movements of construction plant, materials and workforce;

- the duration of the effect.

It is recognised that it is often difficult to provide accurate and complete information on all these varied aspects of a development. Nevertheless, the importance of such information cannot be over-stressed, as it is the foundation for all predictions of effects. It also assists the overall design process and leads to the best and most sustainable environmental solution. Where key data on project characteristics is lacking, there may be a need to make explicit assumptions as to what will happen, based on the 'worst-case situation' or on a range of options. The source of information on the potential effects on landscape and visual amenity must also be clearly set out. Prior to finalising the Environmental Statement, assumptions should be checked to ensure they are still applicable and updated in the light of any new data. 4.14

Integration

Within the context of the iterative process of environmental appraisal, landscape planning, design and impact assessment, the information about the development is examined and the design refined to avoid, reduce or offset likely negative or adverse landscape and visual effects. Those elements that continue to give rise to likely effects on the landscape and on visual amenity can be identified, described in detail and integrated into the wider framework of impact assessment. Part 6 addresses this process in more detail. 4.15

The development proposals, which are common to all topics addressed in the ES, are usually described in a separate section. Only those key elements giving rise to effects on the landscape and visual amenity need to be addressed in the assessments of landscape and visual impact. The development proposals are generally illustrated in simple, easy-to-read proposal maps at A3 or A4 size, together with other selected drawings such as cross sections. For complex projects, or for those of 4.16

a long duration such as power stations or major mineral workings, a series of drawings at different stages such as construction, operation and decommissioning, or phases in the development may be needed. Essential illustrations include:

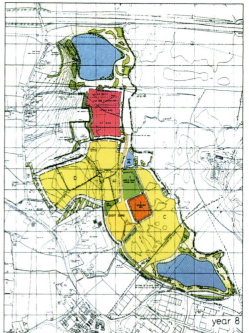

operations

working area

plant area & access

topsoil & peat storage area

overburden store

silt settlement area

soil screening bunds

water ponds

landscape

preplanting area

existing hedgerows

existing trees to be kept

areas of shrub planting

areas of tree planting

water - with shallows

grass

Using clear and concise graphic techniques this series of drawings communicates the sequence of parallel operations where minerals are extended and a new landscape is formed

- layout plans of the main design elements, including access and site circulation, land uses, contours and site levels;

- cross sections and elevations of buildings and other important structures where available, including key dimensions;

- the proposed landscape framework including landform and planting.

Information on presentation techniques is given in Part 8.

In this example, appropriate colour treatment of the buildings has been used to help the structures fit in with the landscape

Furzey Island in Dorset, part of the BP Wytch Farm Complex. Extensive screening results in a development with minimal visual impact but nevertheless has landscape impact on the landscape character of the area

Part 5

Mitigation

Introduction

The purpose of **mitigation** is to avoid, reduce and where possible remedy or offset, any significant negative (adverse) effects on the environment arising from the proposed development.

5.1

Mitigation is thus not solely concerned with 'damage limitation' but may also consider measures that could compensate for unavoidable residual effects. If good environmental planning and design principles are applied, together with a flexible approach to design, a high degree of mitigation can be built into the scheme from the outset, which can thereby reduce the extent or scale of adverse effects.

5.2

Mitigation measures may be considered under two categories:

5.3

- primary measures that intrinsically comprise part of the development design through an iterative process;

- secondary measures designed to specifically address the remaining (residual) negative (adverse) effects of the final development proposals.

Mitigation measures are generally more effective if they are designed as an integral part of an iterative process of project planning and design. Mitigation is thus used as a design approach that is, where possible, implemented from project inception when alternative designs or site options are being considered. In such circumstances it can be used to adapt and modify the development to take account of constraints and opportunities, and achieve the optimum environmental fit as part of an environmentally integrated design.

5.4

Primary mitigation measures that form integrated mainstream components of the project design are included in the project description. This should focus on factual explanation of the basic design elements – such as siting, access, layout, buildings, structures, ground modelling and planting – in so far as they affect landscape and visual resources. The design philosophy can also describe the benefits to the design of alternative solutions, introduced to reduce potential negative effects, and indicate how these have been addressed.

5.5

Secondary measures designed specifically for mitigation of the negative effects of the final development are considered in the assessment of landscape and visual effects. They also meet any formal requirement to identify measures for the avoidance or reduction of negative effects.

5.6

Landscape proposals that are most likely to be a long-term success are those which meet the environmental objectives and any technical, locational or financial development constraints. It is also important to demonstrate that long-term control and management is secured, including 'off-site' measures such as habitat

5.7

restoration or planting, proposed on land outside the developer's control, to mitigate a localised negative change in visual amenity. The aim is to effect an overall benefit to landscape character, condition and value, while offsetting any negative environmental effects.

Strategies to address likely negative (adverse) effects

5.8 The *ideal* strategy for each identifiable negative effect is one of avoidance. If this is not possible, alternative strategies of reduction, remediation and compensation may each be explored. If the consideration of mitigation measures for negative landscape or visual effects is left to the later stages of scheme design, this can result in increased mitigation costs, because early opportunities for avoidance of negative effects are missed. Thus remediation and compensation of residual negative effects are generally less cost effective than avoidance. Some of the main issues associated with the different mitigation strategies are outlined below.

Avoidance

5.9 Avoidance of negative landscape and visual effects can be achieved through careful siting, planning and design. For almost every major development, time, costs and public concern can be reduced if serious environmental constraints can be identified and avoided during the development of the planning and design of the scheme. This may be achieved through the selection of a site that can more readily accommodate the proposed development, or through innovative design.

Reduction

5.10 Where negative effects cannot be avoided, the reduction of any remaining conflict with the landscape and other environmental constraints requires detailed consideration of site characteristics. Setting a development into the ground can often help it to be integrated into the landscape. New landforms and planting, as part of mitigation measures, can increase the ability of the landscape to accommodate development, always provided that they are in keeping with the character of the area and are appropriate to the specific circumstances. However, poorly-designed new landscape features can give rise to negative landscape or visual effects.

Remediation

5.11 Mitigation measures that rely solely on 'add-on' or 'cosmetic' landscape measures such as screen planting to remedy the negative effects of an otherwise fixed scheme design, are likely to be the least successful. Nevertheless, the sympathetic treatment of external areas should augment the integration of a

new development with the surrounding landscape. Remediation should be seen
as part of the overall process of avoiding and reducing adverse impacts.

Compensation

Where a negative effect cannot be mitigated to an acceptable degree, other compen- 5.12
satory measures or related environmental improvements may offset or compensate
for unavoidable residual effects. For compensation to be effective, a reliable assessment is needed of the nature, value and extent of the resource that would be lost, so
that like can be replaced with like or, where this is not possible, measures of equivalent value are provided. However, it is questionable that true compensation is ever
possible as, for example, a new area of woodland may eventually – over several
decades – compensate for the loss of an existing mature woodland in purely visual
terms, but may never compensate for the loss of established habitat or amenity
value. In general, compensation should be regarded as a last resort. Where habitat
creation is attempted, expert advice should always be sought.

Increasingly, compensation may be offered or sought by local communities or 5.13
local authorities as an 'appeasement' for unavoidable negative effects due to the
scale or character of a new development. Such measures may include off-site
planting carried out in the gardens of affected properties to screen negative views
of a development, the provision of new local amenity areas or parks, or the
creation or provision of a work of art as part of or separate from the development. These measures need not be associated with issues of 'planning gain'.

Enhancement

The landscape and visual impact assessment may identify measures to manage 5.14
necessary change (arising from the development), while maintaining and, where
possible, enhancing the quality of the environment for local people and visitors
(see Appendix 2 and PPG 7 para 3.1).

Although often linked to mitigation, enhancement is a separate issue that 5.15
explores the opportunities and appropriateness for a development project to
contribute positively to the landscape of the development site and its wider
setting. Enhancement proposals are based on a sound initial assessment of landscape character, quality and trends for change in which the following questions
may be addressed:

- Can the development help restore or reconstruct local landscape character
  and local distinctiveness?

- Can it assist in meeting regulatory authority landscape management objectives for the area?

- Can it help solve specific issues such as derelict land reclamation?

5.16 Enhancement may take many forms, including improved land management, or restoration of historic landscapes, habitats and other valued features; enrichment of denuded agricultural landscapes; measures to conserve and improve the attractiveness of town centres; and creation of new landscape, habitat and recreational areas. Such measures allow environmental enhancement to make a very real contribution to sustainable development and the overall quality of the environment.

Guidelines for mitigation

5.17 The application of the following good practice principles can increase the effectiveness of the mitigation measures in that:

- All negative (adverse) landscape and visual effects that are likely to occur throughout the project life cycle – including construction, operation, decommissioning and restoration – should be considered for mitigation, although the statutory requirement is limited to significant effects.

- Consultation with local community and special interest groups on the proposed mitigation measures is important and can also be helpful in identifying local needs and preferences.

- Landscape mitigation measures should be designed to suit the existing landscape character and needs of the locality, respecting and building on local landscape distinctiveness and helping to address any relevant existing issues in the landscape.

- It must be recognised that many mitigation measures, especially planting, are not immediately effective. Advance planting can help to reduce the time between the development commencing and the planting becoming established. Where planting is intended to provide a visual screen for the development, it may also be appropriate to assess residual effects for different periods of time, such as day of opening, year five and year fifteen.

- The developer should demonstrate a commitment to the implementation of mitigation measures to an agreed programme and budget. Responsibility for the implementation of all the mitigation measures (normally the developer) should be clearly defined.

- The proposed mitigation measures should address specific issues, and performance standards should be identified for the establishment, management, maintenance and monitoring of new landscape features, describing exactly what is required for mitigation to be effective. This could be achieved through a method statement, which could also incorporate contingency plans, in the event that mitigation measures prove to be unsuccessful.

- A programme of appropriate monitoring may be agreed with the regulatory authority so that compliance and effectiveness can be readily monitored and evaluated.

Box 5.1   Common mitigation measures

- **Sensitive location and siting** can offer significant opportunities for effective mitigation, through choice of site and location within the site.
- **Site layout:** careful consideration of the site layout can help to reduce landscape or visual effects. For example, buildings can be located to screen unsightly features or activities from a sensitive viewpoint.
- **Choice of site level:** landscape is three-dimensional and can provide scope for reducing adverse effects in the careful choice of site level or vertical alignment.
- **Appropriate form, materials and design of built structures:** many buildings and structures cannot be screened; nor is it always desirable or practicable to do so. In these circumstances, the design of the structures themselves, their colour treatment and textual finishes, can be designed to fit comfortably with their surroundings.
- **Lighting** for safety or security purposes is often unavoidable and can give rise to considerable adverse visual effects. Modern lighting designs are now available to minimise or avoid upward and lateral light pollution by design of the lantern, directional fittings, or screening the light source by the use of baffles. It is also possible to minimise the use of lighting with systems that light the minimum area required to be lit for the minimum period of time.
- **Ground modelling** may be undertaken where the natural landform or site levels do not give optimum screening effect. However, major earthworks in themselves may create adverse landscape and visual effects, and care is required to ensure that new landforms look natural and appear as an integral part of the landscape.
- **Planting:** structural planting can help to integrate a development with the surrounding landscape, and can soften the edges of intrusive buildings and structures. Where possible, the planting should be appropriate to the landscape reflecting local species of national provenance. Advance planting and, where appropriate, off-site planting, offer particular potential for effective mitigation.
- **Use of camouflage or disguise:** visual effects may be reduced by changing the perceived appearance of a development or structure to one that may be more visually acceptable to the local community, or one that fits more readily into the landscape.

Case study

Felsted Sugar Beet Factory	
Felsted Essex	
February 2001	
Principal author: Novell Tullett	

CONTEXT	
Urban fringe/rural	

DETAILS OF PROPOSAL

Summary description	Scheme for 650 new houses, 25 hectares of landscape setting and new nature reserve on derelict sugar beet works site.
Nature and scope of issues	Scale: Comprehensive large-scale site including factory buildings, silos and 50 hectares of derelict land.
	Sensitivity: High; set within an SLA and including a main river and tributary and a local nature reserve.
	Policy: Topical; PPG 3 sequential approach, weaknesses outweighed by net environmental benefits.
Planning/ regulatory content	Sustainability issues in PPGs 3, 7 and 13; design issues in PPGs 1 and 3.
	Located in countryside within an SLA.
	Consultation with Environment Agency on river flood and conservation issues, and with English Nature on nature conservation issues.
	Essex Design Guide.
	Local plan allocation as a sustainable urban extension.

CASE ANALYSIS

Approach	The principal objectives were to structure the housing development with reference to the morphology of traditional Essex villages; to avoid impact on sensitive countryside; and to employ the 50 hectares of reclamation to a new landscape setting to reverse the negative effect of the former industry on the SLA and river valleys.
Methodology	GLVIA, Essex Design Guide.
Application of methodology	Desktop studies, field work, computer modelling (AutoCAD), Photoshop, aerial photography, 50mm photography, photomontage, public consultation and evidence at Local Plan Inquiry. The landscape architect led the master-planning stage, which involved co-ordinating planning, transport and engineering issues with the design objectives.

CRITIQUE/CONCLUSIONS

Critique	Site has a range of difficult constraints. Investigations included topographical models, gas generation monitoring, Stage 2 habitat surveys, river corridor habitat surveys, floodplain modelling, sewage treatment works, *cordon sanitaire* (air quality), archaeological investigations and landscape and visual impact assessment. Combined computer and traditional methods successful at technical level (Public Inquiry evidence, ES) but hard to convey to public.
Solution	Planning issues report: a less technical document than ES to explain design in response to issues and planning gain (improved landscape, visual amenity and nature conservation). Public exhibition explained important issues and tested preferences for options. Outline consent used to create setting for new village structure, and to set out design brief for new housing layout and design. House-builders helped interpret brief in detailed planning applications and ensured design philosophy and objectives were maintained. Sustainability initiatives included re-use of 200,000 m³ of reclaimed material on site giving benefit from re-use of brownfield land.
Conclusion	Authorities persuaded of benefits of proposals through investigation and analysis with positive, beneficial plans for environmental improvement.

Case study

Landscape Strategy for Truro, Falmouth and Penryn
Cornwall

December 2000
Client: Carrick District Council
Principal author: Landscape Design Associates

CONTEXT

Urban/urban fringe The settlements of Truro, Falmouth and Penryn
Rural Their immediate landscape setting

Truro, topography

DETAILS OF PROPOSAL

Summary description	The preparation of a landscape strategy for Truro, Falmouth and Penryn to guide the identification of potential directions of growth and development within the rural areas surrounding the three principal towns in Carrick District.
Nature and scope of issues	Analysis of towns within their landscape setting. Integrated townscape and landscape assessment. Evaluation of local landscape character areas and assessment of development capacity. Identification of potential directions for growth and development sites. Guidelines and principles for the design of development.
Planning/ regulatory content	To inform the review of the Carrick District Wide Local Plan.

CASE ANALYSIS

Approach	A robust and transparent approach was required to withstand close scrutiny within the Local Plan Review process.
Methodology	Baseline study and analysis of the landscape and townscape character and setting of each town. Evaluation of the overall sensitivity and potential of each character area to accommodate change. This involved an assessment of the impacts upon the following three factors, with the degree of impact graded according to the classifications indicated: • The intrinsic character and quality of the receiving landscape: high, moderate or low. • The setting and character of the town: critical, supportive, connective or beyond setting. • Visual prominence and intervisibility: high, moderate or low. A matrix of the findings of the impact assessment on these three factors informed the evaluation of the overall sensitivity of each character area, and the potential for development.

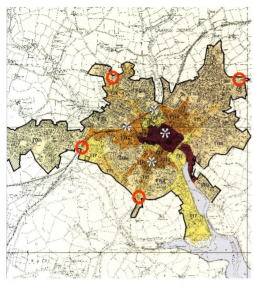

Truro, townscape character areas

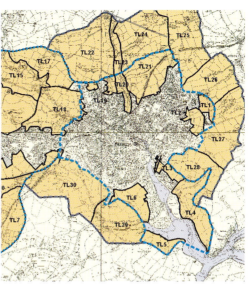

Truro, landscape character areas and potential for development

Character Areas	Intrinsic Quality			Role in Setting of Town				Visual Characteristics						Overall Sensitivity and Potential for Development						
								Visual Prominence			Intervisibility			Overall Sensitivity			Development Potential			
	High	Moderate	Low	Critical	Supportive	Connective	Beyond Setting	High	Mod	Low	High	Mod	Low	High	Mod	Low	Suitable	Some Potential	V.Limited Potential	Unsuitable
1		•		•				•			•				•					•
2			•			•			•				•		•		•	•		
3		•		•				•			•				•					•
4	•			•				•				•		•						•
5	•			•				•				•		•						•
6		•		•				•			•			•						•
7		•				•			•			•			•					•
8	•					•			•		•			•						•
9		•				•		•				•			•					•
10	•					•				•		•	•	•						•

Extract from table summarising landscape evaluation and identification of potential for development

CRITIQUE/CONCLUSIONS

Critique	The success of the methodology relies on a clearly defined, systematic approach, with a comprehensive baseline study and analysis guiding the integrated landscape and townscape assessment and identification of local landscape character areas. These provide the framework for the assessment of potential impact and evaluation of overall sensitivity and development capacity.
	The matrix analysis of the factors that contribute to sensitivity provides a clearly identifiable format for representing the evaluation of overall sensitivity, and analysing and identifying potential development areas.

Case study

Land at Downton Road, Salisbury
Salisbury, Wiltshire

November 1999
Principal author: Landscape Design Associates

CONTEXT

Urban fringe

Setting of Salisbury, topography

DETAILS OF PROPOSAL

Summary description	Promotion of a 38 acre site for housing development on the southern perimeter of Salisbury through the Local Plan Review.
Nature and scope of issues	Setting of city: Evaluation of landscape and townscape character areas and impact of development of site on the setting of the city.
	Capacity assessment: Categorisation of areas of influence within Salisbury and setting; determination of capacity to accept development.
	Comparative assessment of impact of development: Appraisal of site and other allocated sites and evaluation of impact.
Planning/ regulatory content	The impact assessment formed part of the proof of evidence prepared for presentation at Salisbury District Local Plan Inquiry on behalf of Westbury Homes.

CASE ANALYSIS

Approach	The study's main purpose was to demonstrate the acceptability of the landscape and visual impact of residential development within an area of land on the southern perimeter of Salisbury in the context of the wider setting of the city. An appraisal of Salisbury's setting was undertaken to evaluate the landscape's capacity to accept development and minimise adverse impacts.
Methodology	Baseline study including a topographical analysis, identification of the planning context and a Landscape Character Assessment. This informed the analysis stage and guided the evaluation of the areas of influence within the setting of Salisbury. Landscape and townscape character areas were classified into visually cohesive or visually fragmented in respect of the historic core, and distinctive, supportive and connective townscape/landscape within the remainder of the study area. These findings guided the identification of the capacity of each character area to accommodate change, and provided a basis for a comparative analysis of the capacity of the site with other potential development areas.

Salisbury's setting: landscape planning context

Salisbury's setting: landscape character areas

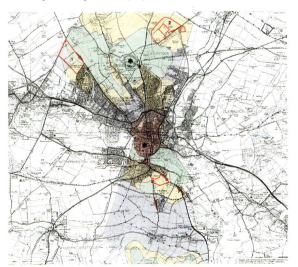

Salisbury's setting: capacity assessment

Salisbury's setting: site context

CRITIQUE/CONCLUSIONS

Critique	The identification of the capacity of an area to accept development relies on a robust and defendable methodology. Thorough and systematic baseline study and analysis informed:
	The identification of townscape and landscape character areas and the distribution of areas of influence within the setting of the city.
	The evaluation of the overall sensitivity and capacity of the landscape to accept development.
	These findings guided the comparative assessment of alternative sites and provided a sound and defendable basis for promoting the site.

Case study

NEWLINCS Integrated Waste Management Facility
Stallingborough, Lincolnshire

April 2000
Client: NEWLINCS Development Ltd
Principal author: Landscape Design Associates

CONTEXT

Urban/urban fringe   Located between Immingham and Grimsby on flat coastal plain. Visually dominated by concentration of existing industrial buildings

Rural   Surrounding area agricultural, but dominant influence of existing industrial structures diminishes site's rural character

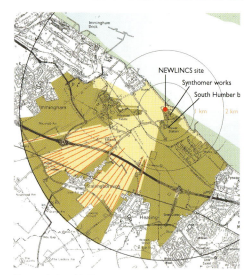

Zone of visual influence

DETAILS OF PROPOSAL

Summary description	Development of an integrated waste management facility including: Energy from waste plant with combined heat and power capability. Composting facility for green waste. Recycling facilities for glass, plastic, cans and paper waste.
Nature and scope of issues	The primary issues were air quality and natural heritage. Despite the size of the proposals, the location meant that landscape was not a primary issue.
Planning/ regulatory content	Production of the ES to accompany the planning application to North East Lincolnshire Council.

CASE ANALYSIS

Approach	Baseline studies demonstrated the site's openness and extensive views. Industrial buildings dominate the flat landscape and significantly diminish the character of the rural landscape; large-scale planting and earthworks would be inappropriate and ineffectual. The main mitigation measures were the building's architectural elements, the main factor in determining impact.
Methodology	CCP423, CCP326 and GLVIA
Application of methodology	Detailed computer modelling of both landform and height of tree cover to establish the precise extent of the required accommodation works..
Presentation	Plan and map-based information within ES and non-technical summary. Photographs and photomontage.

Existing view looking north east from level crossing

Photomontage view, trees shown at 5m on 2m earthbound

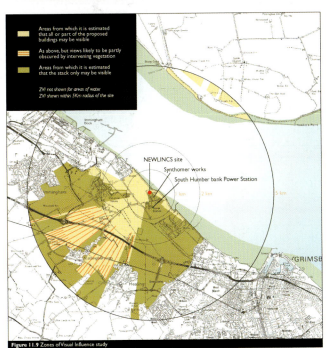

Zone of visual influence

CRITIQUE/CONCLUSIONS

Critique	Use of photomontage and ZVI work, which distinguished between the stack and the remainder of the development, meant that the precise nature of any impact was properly communicated.

Case study

Farnborough Aerodrome
Farnborough, Hampshire

September 1999
Client: TAG Aviation
Principal author: Terence O'Rourke plc

CONTEXT

Urban/urban fringe   Immediately west of Farnborough's urban centre

Rural   The aerodrome extends across a broad swathe of landscape types including both urban and rural

Master plan

DETAILS OF PROPOSAL

Summary description	Expansion and upgrading of civil airline facilities on former MoD airfield. Extension of runway, new passenger terminal and hangars. Continuing provision for the biennial Airshow.
Nature and scope of issues	Visual, landscape character and the impact of new facilities. Effects of aircraft landing and take off safety zones on surrounding land, vegetation and buildings. Nature conservation issues and opportunities arising from required changes to landform and tree cover.
Planning/ regulatory content	The planning application including ES to Rushmoor Borough Council. Civil Aviation Authority licensing requirements.

CASE ANALYSIS

Approach	To demonstrate acceptability of visual impact of a new Substation building from any viewpoint within the Study Area and at a variety of different ground levels. The concept of 'relative scale' needed to be explained to nearby residents to demonstrate that a new 45 m tower could appear relatively smaller than a nearer, existing 35 m tower.
Methodology	CCP423, CCP326 and GLVIA
Application of methodology	Detailed computer modelling of both landform and height of tree cover to establish precise extent of required accommodation works.
Presentaion	Plan and map-based information within the ES and non-technical summary. Photographs and photomontage. Very complex computer modelling in the ES was shown in a format (photographs and plans) designed to give greater clarity to a largely non-technical audience.

Location of hangar and control tower

Location of hangar and control tower with photomontage of proposals

Distance from control tower

ZVI for control tower

CRITIQUE/CONCLUSIONS

Critique	Detailed computer studies within a user-friendly document facilitated a very readable ES, allowing complex issues to be clearly conveyed.

Case study

Coal Clough Wind Farm Extension
Cliviger, Lancashire

December 1999, January 2001
Client: Renewable Energy Systems
Principal author: Landscape Design
Associates

CONTEXT

Urban fringe   Hilltop site that contributes
to the setting of the town of Burnley

Rural   Located within open landscape of
the South Pennines

Photomontage of proposed extension from nearby
viewpoint at similar altitude to site. Variations in
turbine height not especially apparent due to the
effects of perspective

DETAILS OF PROPOSAL

Summary description	Two alternative configurations for the extension of an existing 24-turbine wind farm by three additional larger turbines.
Nature and scope of issues	Extension: The impact of three additional turbines on an existing wind farm cluster of 24. Height: The effect of a 50 per cent increase in new turbines' height on visibility. Variation: The degree to which larger turbines with a slower rotation speed would affect the unified appearance of the existing wind farm. Cumulative effects: The contribution of the extended site to the presence of wind farms within the South Pennine Moors landscape.
Planning/ regulatory content	Contribution to the EIA accompanying the planning application and the subsequent hearing statement at appeal location within the Standing Conference of South Pennine Authorities (SCOSPA) Heritage Area and an Area of Special Landscape Proximity to the Pennine Bridleway National Trail and Burnley Way Recreational Footpath.

CASE ANALYSIS

Approach	Landscape character established by reference to the published SCOSPA Heritage Area Landscape Assessment and confirmed on site. A viewpoint assessment (locations agreed with Burnley Borough Council) investigated the appearance of the extended wind farm from various distances and altitudes.
Methodology	Computer-generated wireframe images of the two alternative configurations were produced. Additional turbines shown in different colours. Reference to the wireframes during site visits enabled the assessor to accurately predict the view and assess the likely impact of the additional larger turbines. Existing turbines acted as reference points within the landscape. Videomontage helped assess the effects of variation in rotation speed.
Presentation	Photographs of the existing view, the wireframes and photomontages of selected key views. Juxtaposition of the existing view and the wireframes provided a clear impression of the potential view.

Existing view

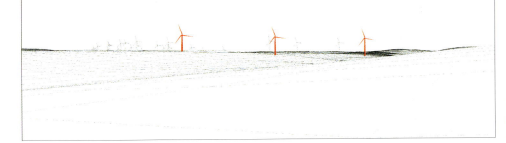

Wireframe of the proposed western option

Wireframe of the proposed southern option

CRITIQUE/CONCLUSIONS

Critique	Juxtaposition of photographs of existing view and wireframes help the assessor overcome problems caused by poor visibility and adverse weather conditions that can hinder production of high-quality photomontage images. Production of wireframes based on a computer model enabled investigation of the wind farm's appearance from different viewpoints. Reference to the real view was always essential to identify whether landscape elements acting as visual reference points for scale were present in the view.
Variation	Full investigation of subtle differences in altitude/variations in ground level/distance/perspective made to degree turbine height variations are apparent.
Cumulative effects	Demonstrated that additional turbines would integrate well with the existing cluster, that variations in their size and rotation speed would not generally be apparent, and that the site's contribution to potential cumulative effects in the area was unlikely to be significantly greater than the existing cluster.

Case study

Portobello Wastewater Treatment Works and Sludge Recycling Centre
Portobello, East Sussex

February 1999
Client: Southern Water plc
Principal author: Terence O'Rourke plc

The proposals

CONTEXT

Urban/Urban fringe   Site located within coastal belt of suburban development between Brighton and Newhaven

Rural   One of the few remaining open areas where the South Downs AONB extends to the coast

DETAILS OF PROPOSAL

Summary description	Replacement of existing headworks with new wastewater treatment works and sludge recycling centre.
	Preparation of full ES for the proposals.
	Preparation of Proofs of Evidence for Section 78 Inquiry.
Nature and scope of issues	Scale: Large-scale industrial facility on 9.4 hectares within cliff recess and foreshore platform.
	Sensitivity: High. Partially within South Downs AONB and SSSI covering the cliffs and cliff tops with extensive coastal views.
Planning/ regulatory content	Need to conform with EU wastewater directive (91/27/EER).
	Consideration given to PPGs 7, 9, 15, 16, 17 and 20.
	Located in Sussex Downs AONB, Countryside Gap and SSSI.

CASE ANALYSIS

Approach	Aim to safeguard character and views to and from the AONB and from local residences by the design of the foreshore platform, the arrangement of buildings and the retention of the cliff.
Methodology	CCP423, CCP326 and GLVIA
Application of methodology	Desktop studies, fieldwork, computer modelling, Photoshop, aerial and 50mm photography, MiniCad, Vectorworks 3D and exaggerated sections.
Presentation	Plan and map-based information within the ES and non-technical summary. Photographs and photomontage. Complex computer modelling within the ES shown clearly, making it readily understood by a non-technical audience.

View 4

View 4 with
photomontage of
proposals
superimposed

Computer-
generated 3D
image and
corresponding
exaggerated
vertical section

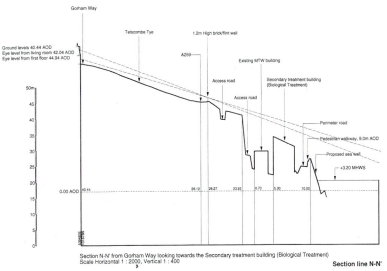

Section N-N' from Gorham Way looking towards the Secondary treatment building (Biological Treatment)
Scale Horizontal 1 : 2000, Vertical 1 : 400

Section line N-N'

CRITIQUE/CONCLUSIONS

Critique	Combination of traditional and computer studies provided good accurate results. Limitations of OS level data are overcome by additional on-site topographic study. Exaggerated long sections were an accurate method for assessing views. 3D computer-generated images add clarity to the results.

Part 6

Baseline studies

Introduction

The initial step in any landscape or visual impact assessment is to review the existing landscape and visual resource – that is, the baseline landscape and visual conditions. The data collected will form the basis from which the occurrence, estimation of magnitude and significance of the landscape and visual effects of the development may be identified and assessed.   6.1

The purpose of baseline studies is to record and analyse the existing landscape features, characteristics, the way the landscape is experienced, and the value or importance of the landscape and visual resources in the vicinity of the proposed development. This requires research, classification and analysis of the landscape and visual resources as follows: 6.2

- **Research/survey** involves both desk and field studies to assemble basic information.

- **Classification** entails sorting landscape into units or groups of distinct and recognisable type and character.

- **Analysis** involves the detailed examination of the constituent parts of the landscape and visual resources in order to understand how they are made up and experienced. It can also include the process of ascertaining the relative importance of the various aspects of the landscape and visual resource.

- **Presentation of findings**.

Methods and tools

The level of detail provided should be appropriate to the scale and type of development, the sensitivity of the receptors and the potential for adverse (negative) or beneficial (positive) effects to occur. It should also be appropriate to each stage of the assessment process. Thus at the scoping and site selection stage, the primary aim is to identify key issues and constraints. For this purpose, a fairly broad-brush, preliminary site assessment with mainly desk-based studies may be adequate, based on landscape designations, existing landscape character assessments, areas of ancient woodland, and known sites of recreational interest that will influence site selection. Once the preferred site has been selected, more comprehensive and detailed baseline studies are carried out. The level of detail required must suit the purpose of each stage.   6.3

Landscape and visual baseline studies play an important part not only in the assessment process but also in the design process, providing an overview of the environmental constraints or opportunities that may influence the design of the final development. It is important that the information collated is considered in   6.4

relation to that for other parallel studies such as cultural heritage and flora and fauna to ensure an integrated approach to design development. Principal sources of background information include the regulatory authority, government agencies and local special interest groups and organisations.

6.5　It is important to bear in mind that the baseline landscape is not static. The landscape may already be changing for reasons unrelated to the development. The baseline studies therefore address not only the existing landscape, but also such landscape dynamics as may be identified, together with the likely future character of the landscape without the proposed development. Account is also taken of any landscape management strategy or guidelines that exist or are in preparation for the area of study. The baseline studies are a strict record and analysis of the existing landscape and visual resources. They must not be confused or combined with impact analysis, which is not attempted at this stage. The following sections consider separately the landscape and visual baselines in more detail.

Landscape baseline

6.6　When commencing a landscape impact assessment, it is essential to visit the site in order to review and supplement existing map and written data about the development site and surrounding area. These studies may initially extend well beyond the development site, both to assist in site selection, and to help establish and understand the wider landscape setting and context.

Area of study

6.7　When deciding on the area of study, it is important to distinguish between the study of the physical landscape and the study of visual amenity. The former will address the site itself and its wider landscape context, within which the proposed development may influence landscape character.

Desk study

6.8　Information of relevance to the proposed development is extracted and summarised, either as written text or in map form. In particular, the desk study explores:

- **patterns** and scale of **landform**, **land cover**, **land use** and **built development**, which give guidance on the general landscape character of the surrounding area, and lead to the definition of character areas;

- **any special values** that may apply, for example, those recognised by international designation or treaty, national (statutory) landscape designation, local (non-statutory) landscape designations and Conservation Areas or features of architectural importance;

- **special interests** including nature conservation, historical or cultural heritage associations;

- other **professional evaluations** or studies on the landscape within the study area;

- past and present perceptions of **local value** available from the regulatory authority, local amenity groups/residents.

Box 6.1 Useful sources of information

Useful sources of information include

- Supplementary or informal planning documents such as countryside strategies and landscape character assessments or guidelines; current and historical Ordnance Survey and other maps.
- Geology, soils and land use maps, hydrological survey.
- Vertical aerial photographs.
- Structure and local plans showing landscape designations, Conservation Areas and other relevant planning policies (including associated environmental survey and issues reports).
- National planning policy guidance.
- National Parks and AONB management plans.
- Data on archaeology, ecology and buildings and settlements and other conservation interests within the area.
- Common Land and Rights of Way maps.
- Meteorological Office data.
- Site plans including topographical survey, tree condition survey, development plans.

6.9 The desk study provides a sound basis for subsequent field surveys. It may also help in defining draft landscape character areas for the landscape surrounding the development and highlight sensitive receptors.

Field survey

6.10 Information collated in the desk study requires confirmation in the field, particularly in urban and urban fringe settings where map and even data from aerial photography may be out of date. On larger projects it may be helpful for the field survey to be carried out by more than one person to facilitate discussion and obtain a consensus view between professionals as part of the process of verification.

6.11 A common technique for field survey and assessment of landscape character involves the completion of a structured field survey report, based upon observations recorded from selected viewpoints across the study area, using a standard survey form. The viewpoints selected should provide representative coverage of the area including, where relevant, how it is experienced. The survey form permits recording of both objective description and subjective impressions of the landscape, as well as details of landscape condition, land use, management and trends for change. If the development is likely to result in different noise types or levels, the current noise status should also be recorded. Units of common landscape character may be defined from analysis of the findings of the field and desk studies (see [4], where Countryside Agency publications provide more detailed advice on survey forms).

Sensitive receptors

6.12   The field survey identifies and records specific sensitive receptors. The term 'receptor' is used in landscape and visual impact assessments to mean an element or assemblage of elements that will be directly or indirectly affected by the proposed development.

6.13   Landscape receptors include elements of the physical landscape that may be directly affected by the development such as topographic, geological and drainage features; woodland, tree and hedgerow cover; land use; field boundaries and artefacts. The importance and value of landscape receptors should also be established where practicable.

Landscape elements (including features)	• Trees, woodlands, hedgerows, meadows. • Landform and topographic features, e.g. open hill tops, coastlines, valleys, open green space, etc. • River corridors, streams, ponds, lakes and rivers. • Built elements, e.g. walls, paved squares, bridges, walks, parks, buildings, roads.
Landscape characteristics (tangible and intangible)	• Characteristic patterns and combinations of landscape features including landform, landcover and cultural elements which contribute to landscape character. • Scenic quality. • Sense of place (genius loci). • Tranquillity or wildness qualities.
Landscape character	The distinct and recognisable pattern of elements that occurs consistently in a particular type of landscape, and how this is perceived by people. It reflects particular combinations of geology, landform, soils, vegetation, land use and human settlement. It creates the particular sense of place of different areas of the landscape.

Figure 6.1   Examples of landscape receptors

Landscape baseline analysis

The analysis draws upon the information gathered during the desk study and 6.14 field survey work, supported by illustrations and documentary evidence. The baseline studies section of the report covers the existing elements, features, characteristics, character, quality and extent of the landscape. The baseline studies and analysis must be clearly explained in the assessment. The findings should be presented in a clear and structured fashion as they form a key component of the landscape and visual impact assessments. A distinction is made between:

- the description and assessment of the individual elements, features, and characteristics of a landscape and their value or importance; and

- analysis of the way in which these components interact to create the character of the landscape.

Landscape character and characterisation

Landscape character assessment and particularly the stage of characterisation is 6.15 the basic tool for understanding the landscape and is the starting point for baseline surveys. There is a well-established methodology developed in the UK by the Countryside Agency and Scottish Natural Heritage [4]. The baseline report provides a concise description of the existing character of the site and its surrounding landscape, including the physical and human influences that have helped to shape the landscape and any current trends for change. This will often include, as appropriate, a classification of the landscape into distinct character areas or types, which share common features and characteristics. It may also take into account other landscape character assessments that may have been prepared for the study area. The description of character may be illustrated by photographs or analytical sketches, or both, showing representative views.

Landscape condition

The condition of the landscape refers to the state of an individual area of land- 6.16 scape and is described as factually as possible. Reference to the maintenance and condition of individual elements or features such as buildings, hedgerows, woodland or drainage systems can be helpful. It should be recognised that landscapes in poor condition, such as degraded or damaged landscapes, can be still be highly locally valued (see paragraph 6.18), for example, if open land is scarce or possibly because of cultural associations, as in the case of sites of industrial archaeological value. The assessment therefore sets out what weight has been attached to the condition of the landscape and may also consider the scope for the development to contribute to the restoration or enhancement of the landscape.

Box 6.2 Landscape character assessment

On a broad scale, the Countryside Agency's and English Nature's joint **Character of England map** (1996) illustrates the natural and cultural characteristics of the English countryside based on biodiversity and landscape. The character map also includes contributions from English Heritage on the historic features of the landscape.

The approach identifies the unique character of different areas of the countryside without making judgements about their relative worth. Broad areas of cohesive character have been identified, which can be described in terms of their landscape character, sense of place, local distinctiveness, characteristic wildlife and natural features, and nature of change [12].

New guidance on *Landscape Character Assessment*, jointly produced by the Countryside Agency and Scottish Natural Heritage, is due to be published in 2002 [4].

In Scotland, Scottish Natural Heritage (SNH) has completed the national programme of **landscape character assessments**. The series of 29 individual reports, mostly at a scale of 1:50,000, was produced in collaboration with local authorities and other relevant bodies. SNH has also identified **Natural Heritage Zones**, which provide a comparable strategic framework, of 21 zones defined on the basis of a combination of aspects of natural heritage and landscape character [13].

On a similar basis the Forestry Commission has developed a method of landscape assessment for use in the preparation of Indicative **Forest Strategies** and the Environment Agency has a closely-related approach for the assessment of river corridors. This includes a **'Macro' scale assessment** of the wider river valley and a **'Micro' scale assessment** of the immediate river corridor. This has also been extended to the assessment of the whole river catchment area in a number of studies in the Thames and Midlands regions of the Environment Agency [14].

The Countryside Council of Wales is currently promoting **LANDMAP**, a method of mapping and evaluating the rural landscape, in terms of the aspects that contribute to the whole. Landmap is used by Welsh planning authorities as the basis for countryside policy making and strategies for development or protection. All these methods provide vocabularies to describe the wider countryside and are important starting points in investigating the landscape resource [15].

Landscape value

6.17 A judgement needs to be made on the value or importance to society of the affected landscape. This will be based on and take into account views of consultees including (if possible) the public, about what is important in a landscape and why. This information is required in order to:

- establish the level of importance of the affected landscape and whether this is at local, regional or national level;

- enable any losses of landscape features, characteristics, or functions to be assessed in relation to the importance or value attached to them;

- enable the effects on other, less tangible, perceptual landscape characteristics to be assessed such as scenic quality, tranquillity or wildness;

- assist in identifying features which could be enhanced;

- identify mitigation proposals, through avoidance or relocation, by appropriate remedy or offsetting negative effects through compensatory measures.

When describing landscape value, it is important to identify the people or groups who could be affected by the proposals because the landscape is valuable to people in different ways. Consideration is therefore given to: 6.18

- people who live or work in an area may have a different perception of the landscape to that held by visitors because of their more regular contact with the landscape and the ongoing changes within it;

- special interests: for example, the ecological, cultural or historic value of the landscape, as knowledge of these issues can often affect peoples' perception and appreciation of the landscape;

- landscapes valued by a wider public than the local population, because they have a strong image or are well known and valued nationally or internationally, such as the Giant's Causeway, Stonehenge, Edinburgh Castle or Trafalgar Square.

For criteria to help determine landscape value see Reference 4. (Further guidance on consultation is given in Part 9 of these guidelines.)

The analysis of landscape value or importance aims to reflect the value of the landscape at a specific scale, identify the group to which it is important and why. The assessment distinguishes between importance at different scales, for example, some features are locally abundant but may be nationally or internationally scarce, or nationally abundant but locally scarce. 6.19

The assessment of landscape importance includes references to policy or designations as an indicator of recognised value. If the site is located in, or close to, a designated landscape, the evaluation also examines the basis of the designation. These include the specific features or characteristics that justified designation of the area, for example, the selection criteria at the time of designation and the 6.20

definition of boundaries, and whether or not the landscape has subsequently changed. This information is needed as part of the baseline to establish why the landscape is considered to be of value at a national, regional or local level.

6.21 The particular characteristics of a designated landscape are unlikely to be spread evenly throughout the designated area. It is therefore important to consider the variations in landscape elements, characteristics and character to establish the contribution or importance of the proposed development site within the designated area. A decision needs to be made as to whether the site is special, distinctive, representative or includes characteristic features. At a local scale, a site may have a landscape value that is different (either more or less important) to that given by formal designation in terms of its contribution to its immediate environment.

Enhancement potential

6.22 The analysis of landscape character helps to determine the potential for landscape enhancement. It may be possible to identify, for example, those landscapes:

- which have a highly distinctive character and sense of place or have many features that are notable, for example, their scenic, historical or ecological interest;

- where individual elements or features have suffered decline, but where there is still scope to restore the current character, or aspects of it;

- where the overall character has been significantly altered, so that reconstruction, or even creation of a new landscape is required.

6.23 These are not rigid distinctions and clearly form part of a continuum of landscape quality and condition. However, such an analysis can give a general indication as to where, and how, new development can be sensitively accommodated in the landscape. It can also indicate important issues of degradation or adverse landscape effects, which may be compensated for through landscape or environmental enhancement or as 'planning gain' associated with new development.

Visual baseline

Area of study

6.24 The area of study for the visual assessment may extend to the whole of the area from which the development is visible (the visual envelope). In practice the extent of the area to be reported on may be limited by agreement with the regulatory authority on the distance from the proposed development within which the view is expected to be of interest or concern.

In open landscapes, where higher ground provides views of the site, the potential visual influence of the proposed development could extend beyond any predetermined limit fixed from map data alone without a site visit. Conversely, within enclosed landscapes with restricted views the potential effect may be concentrated within a smaller area than that previously determined. It is therefore important to define the study area (and scale) for the assessment within the methodology for each individual site and, where possible, agree this with the regulatory authority at the outset.

Desk study

The desk study explores: 6.26

- the nature of the visual amenity of the area along with the approximate **visibility** of the development, which is determined through topographic analysis from contour data, either manually or by computer;

- specific potential **receptors of visual effects**, including residents, visitors, travellers through the area and other groups of viewers;

The desk study provides the basis for subsequent field surveys and may: 6.27

- delineate the likely zone of visual influence;

- identify the principal viewpoints;

- highlight sensitive visual receptors.

Field survey

Site visits provide the opportunity for the landscape professional to become   6.28 familiar with the site and identify landmarks for use as reference points when looking back towards the site from the surrounding landscape. Looking outwards from the site can often be the best or only way of identifying certain viewpoints, for example, residential properties with windows with views of the site or development. The actual **extent of visibility** will need to be checked in the field due to the localised screening effects of buildings, walls, fences, trees, hedgerows and banks. In order to achieve this, knowledge of the precise siting and dimensions of the proposed development is required and artificial landmarks indicating the height and location of proposed structures may also be helpful. When new lighting is a significant part of the proposed development, it may be important to carry out 'dark' night-time surveys of the existing conditions in order to assess potential effects of lighting. The visibility survey will need to be reviewed and updated as siting, layout and design proposals are progressively refined or amended.

Principal **representative viewpoints** within the study area are also identified   6.29 during the site visit, which may include walking public footpaths and bridleways

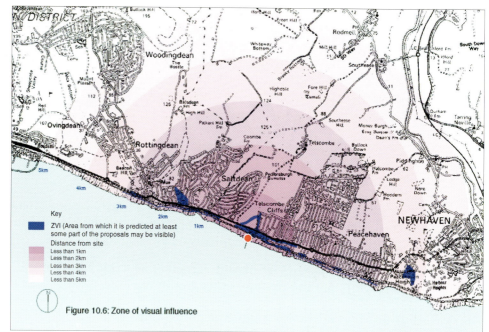

Zone of visual
influence

Figure 10.6: Zone of visual influence

Key

ZVI (Area from which it is predicted at least
some part of the proposals may be visible)

Distance from site
Less than 1km
Less than 2km
Less than 3km
Less than 4km
Less than 5km

Impact of road
lighting and
lights from
passing cars on a
dual carriageway

(making an allowance for the height of horse riders) and visiting areas of open public access. Public viewpoints are clearly important, but private viewpoints may also be relevant and should be considered on site. The visual survey also includes and is supported by a comprehensive photographic record from the principal and other relevant viewpoints.

Visual receptors include the public or community at large, residents, visitors, and other groups of viewers as well as the visual amenity of people affected. Records are produced of the types of viewers affected, an estimate of their numbers where practical and appropriate, duration of view and important views or views of and from valued landscapes. Potential seasonal screening effects should also be identified and recorded.   6.30

Visual amenity of the affected population viewing the landscape

- users of recreational landscapes/public footpaths and bridleways including tourists and visitors;
- residents;
- users of public sports grounds and amenity open space;
- users of public roads, railways;
- workers;
- views of or from within valued landscapes.

Figure 6.2   Examples of visual receptors

Visual baseline analysis

The analysis of the visual baseline information identifies the extent and nature of the existing views of the site from the principal representative viewpoints, and the nature and characteristics of the visual amenity of the potentially sensitive visual receptors.   6.31

The potential extent to which the existing site is visible from surrounding areas can be presented on a plan using visibility mapping techniques such as zones of visual influence, visual envelopes or visual corridors. Elements such as landform, buildings or vegetation that may interrupt, filter or otherwise influence views are also identified. Principal viewpoints are mapped and these views illustrated by photographs and/or sketches, with annotations to describe any important characteristics, and the changes that will arise as a result of the development. The preparation of photomontages may assist in this process. Where photomontages are to be produced, it is useful to seek agreement with the regulatory authority on the viewpoints to be represented.   6.32

| # Case study

National Grid GIS Substation
Northfleet, Kent

June 1999
Principal author: Insite Environments

CONTEXT

Urban fringe
Adjacent to residential area
Prominent hillside location

DETAILS OF PROPOSAL

Summary description	New Gas Insulated Substation and alteration of adjacent transmission towers.
Nature and scope of issues	Scale: Building and associated infrastructure occupies approx. 4 hectares of land. Sensitivity: Medium, but cumulative impacts considered with substantial existing transmission equipment.
Planning/ regulatory content	Virtual reality model and Environmental Report to accompany an application for planning permission.

CASE ANALYSIS

Approach	To demonstrate acceptability of visual impact of a new Substation building from any viewpoint within the Study Area and at a variety of different ground levels. The concept of 'relative scale' needed to be explained to nearby residents to demonstrate that a new 45 m tower could appear relatively smaller than a nearer, existing 35 m tower.
Methodology	Virtual reality modelling with standard photomontage techniques.
Application of methodology	Type/techniques: Field survey, AutoCAD 2000 plans, digital terrain and building modelling, 50 mm photography. Digital projection of interactive 3D models at public and planning meetings to show different options.

CRITIQUE/CONCLUSIONS

Critique	Calibration of the VR model against standard visual impact techniques persuaded people new to virtual reality that the model was an accurate representation of reality. Once confidence in the technique was established, a variety of built options were tested and the screening benefit of planting over time was illustrated. The public found VR enabled them to understand the nature of the development better than static 2D plans.
Flexibility	VR offered the planning authority the ability to: • switch instantly between existing and proposed views from any angle; • examine the influence of other proposed developments; • visualise the effect of incrementally raising and lowering the substation to determine an optimum level to balance visual impact against removal of additional spoil from site.
Additional issues	The VR model also demonstrated that no undue visual impact would result from leaving a substantial volume of fill material on site. This produced other environmental benefits in terms of reduction of dust, fuel consumption, road movements and need for additional landfill capacity.

Case study

Kent Power Station Environmental Impact Assessment
Isle of Grain, Kent

May 1998

Principal author: RSK Environment Ltd

CONTEXT

Coastal   Estuary-side location within a dominantly industrialised area

DETAILS OF PROPOSAL

Summary description	Proposed 1200 MW Combined Cycle Gas Turbine (CCGT) electricity generating station with new National Grid pylons, on reclaimed industrial land of former British Gas storage site, Isle of Grain, Kent.
Nature and scope of issues	Scale: Large-scale industrial facility on 8 hectares, with an approx. max height of 80 m (combined stack height) Sensitivity: Medium – sited within predominantly industrial area subject to ongoing development, local topography generally flat/low lying; extensive long range views from areas of special landscape and high nature conservation value.
Planning/ regulatory content	Designated as 'primarily general industrial use and warehousing' in local plan. Outside industrial area, local plan policies of 'Areas of Special Significance', a 'Special Landscape Area' and an 'Area of Nature Conservation Value.' Environmental Statement required under the Electricity and Pipeline Works (Assessment of Environmental Effects) Regulations 1990.

CASE ANALYSIS

Approach	Principle concern to safeguard views from surrounding open, low-lying areas and local residential properties by the design of the development in keeping with the existing industrial installations and appropriate screen planting.
Methodology	GLVIA.
Application of methodology	Desktop study, detailed site survey, ground level and aerial (digital) photography, computer modelling using AutoCAD 13, Mapinfo, 3D-Studion Viz and Adobe Photoshop. Detailed OS grid references for proposed site boundaries, tall structures including existing and proposed electricity pylons, together with tall structures in close proximity to establish accurate locations and scaling of proposed development. Detailed 3D wire frames provided by engineers to enable detailed colour modelling of turbine halls and stack.

CRITIQUE/CONCLUSIONS

Critique	Use of latest computer technologies and high-quality aerial and ground level images created a very realistic rendering of the proposed development within the existing environment. This assists a more accurate assessment of visual impacts and is extremely useful for public consultation purposes. Photomontage images subsequently used on public information literature and exhibition panels and to support a planning application by the National Grid for provision of additional pylons.

Presentation of findings

6.33 Baseline studies are presented at differing scales according to the detail shown and focus on the landscape context for the development, and visual resources. At this broad scale, presentational materials may include:

- a map of landscape character areas within the zone of visual influence of the development;

- photographs showing the typical appearance of the landscape within each area, together with key views;

- representative views with respect to visual receptors;

- a map or diagram summarising the key issues, where appropriate;

- at a more detailed level, maps to indicate the specific landscape and visual receptors that influence scheme design.

Further guidance on presentation is given in Part 8.

6.34 On completion of the baseline studies, the general nature and extent of potential landscape and visual effects will be apparent and it may be possible to advise on the overall ability of the landscape and visual environment to accommodate the type of development envisaged.

Part 7

Identification and assessment of landscape and visual effects

Introduction

The assessment of effects aims to: 7.1

- identify systematically the likely effects of the development;

- indicate the measures proposed to avoid, reduce, remedy or compensate for those effects (mitigation measures);

- estimate the magnitude of the effects;

- provide an assessment of the nature and significance of these effects in a logical and well-reasoned fashion.

A distinction is drawn between the potential effects addressed during the design   7.2
development of the scheme and the residual effects after the mitigation
measures have been taken into account. In describing the residual effects, the
likely success or typical performance of the mitigation measures, together with
the arrangements to ensure their implementation, should also be considered.

Although impact assessment is the responsibility of developers and their   7.3
advisers, the opinions of the regulatory authority, relevant statutory consultees,
conservation bodies and, where practicable, local residents should be taken into
account. Some agreement may also have been reached with these groups during
scoping in order to identify and focus study or debate on the potentially significant effects (see the sections on consultation in Part 9).

Assessments of both landscape and visual effects are required for most develop-   7.4
ments. There may, however, be occasions when greater attention is placed on
only one aspect, for example, when a development is wholly screened from
public or private views, but nevertheless results in an adverse effect on landscape
elements or landscape character within the site boundary. Alternatively, but less
likely, a development may have significant visual effects, but insignificant landscape effects.

Sources of effects

Landscape and visual effects can arise from a variety of sources and it is impor-   7.5
tant that potential sources of effect arising throughout the life cycle of the development – their extent, scale, timing and duration – are, where possible,
systematically identified. Effects can arise from all types of development,
including:

- changes in land use, for example those arising from mineral extraction, afforestation, recreational use or land drainage;

- the development of buildings and structures such as power stations, industrial estates, roads and housing;

- changes in land management, such as intensification of agricultural use, which can be a vehicle for biological and landscape change;

- changes in production processes and emissions, which are less common, including those from chemical, food and textile industrial plants.

Nature of effects

7.6   Effects can be negative (adverse) or positive (beneficial); direct, indirect, secondary or cumulative and be either permanent or temporary (short, medium or long term). They can also arise at different scales (local, regional or national) and have different levels of significance (local, regional or national).

Direct and indirect effects

7.7   A direct (or primary) effect may be defined as an effect that is directly attributable to a defined element or characteristic of the proposed development, for example, the loss or removal of an element or feature such as a hedgerow or a prominent group of trees.

7.8   An indirect (or secondary) effect is an effect that is not a direct result of the proposed development but is often produced away from the site of the development or as a result of a complex pathway or secondary association. Indirect effects can arise from consequential changes in the landscape or visual amenity that may be delayed in time or located some distance from the source of the effect. For example, alterations to the drainage regime in the vicinity of a site, such as a quarry, could result in changes to the vegetative cover and a consequent change to the landscape character downstream.

7.9   Indirect effects may result from *associated development*, including:

- upgrading of transport infrastructure and new signs;

- associated mineral extraction and waste disposal requirements;

- new or improved off-site utilities such as water and waste water treatment plants, surface water drainage systems, gas pipelines, electricity substations and transmission lines, and telecommunications facilities.

7.10   Longer-term indirect effects, which could potentially arise as a consequence of the development, might include housing development associated with a large new industrial development; retail development in response to a new road junction; or increased recreational activity following improvements to access. Although such issues cannot be addressed in detail due to lack of information, it may be appropriate to acknowledge them in the assessment, particularly where they could form part of the concerns expressed by consultees and the public.

Such longer-term effects will normally be beyond the scope of the detailed assessment and are primarily issues to be dealt with by the regulatory authority as part of the development control and planning process. In such cases the limitations of the assessment should be acknowledged and agreed, where possible, in discussion with the regulatory authority during scoping.   7.11

Cumulative effects

Cumulative landscape and visual effects result from additional changes to the landscape or visual amenity caused by the proposed development in conjunction with other developments (associated with or separate to it), or actions that occurred in the past, present or are likely to occur in the foreseeable future. They may also affect the way in which the landscape is experienced. Cumulative effects may be positive or negative. Where they comprise a range of benefits, they may be considered to form part of the mitigation measures.   7.12

Cumulative effects can also arise from the intervisibility of a range of developments and/or from the combined effects of individual components of the proposed development occurring in different locations or over a period of time. The separate effects of such individual components or developments may not be significant, but together they may create an unacceptable degree of adverse effect on visual receptors within their combined visual envelopes. Intervisibility depends upon general topography, aspect, tree cover or other visual obstruction, elevation and distance, as this affects visual acuity, which is also influenced by weather and light conditions.   7.13

Box 7.1 Examples of cumulative effects

1 The cumulative effects arising from a range of developments can lead to an unacceptable dègree of adverse effect on receptors, within their combined visual envelopes. Such a combined effect may be subtle, far-reaching and irreversible. Such a situation may arise where a restored landscape, left after temporary mineral workings have ceased, may be markedly different in terms of scenic value and character to the original landscape and thereby extend the effects of the development over a considerably longer time scale than the mineral operations themselves. The possibility of such long-term effects will, therefore, also need to be taken into account in subsequent applications for extensions to a mineral development, or a similar but separate development nearby.

2 On large-scale projects, in particular, the duration of construction and decommissioning may be an important consideration. For instance, in relation to power stations, the tallest site structures may be the construction cranes, the effect of which could be underestimated due to their temporary nature and thus assumed to be short term. However construction may last for several years or more. The longer-term landscape or visual effects of decommissioning the site or facility, and subsequent restoration could also be significant. These could arise from demolition activity, which may use the same equipment as is used in construction, but could also result from residual large scale structures such as reactor cores, which may need to remain for many years after the plant has ceased to operate. Where relevant detailed information is unavailable at the time of the assessment, this should be noted in the assessment and assumptions made on the best information available.

3 For schemes which seek to extend an existing development the assessment will be considering those changes in the landscape likely to occur as a result of the extension, because the base line landscape already includes the existing development, such as a motorway, factory or mineral working. Some people may object to this approach because it appears to favour the development as the greatest change (or harm) to the landscape was caused when the initial road or factory was built, which then makes it easier to apply for road widening or more development. Some objectors argue that the change to the landscape should be described by comparing the effects of the extended scheme with the effects of the existing scheme. This methodology requires an impact assessment of the existing development and information about the pre-development landscape. However the emphasis of the assessment process is on the changes the proposal would bring to the existing landscape, to inform the decision-making process. Nevertheless extensions or additions to existing developments do need to take into account changes of scale and the potential for the receiving landscape to accommodate the larger composite feature. This may be addressed in an assessment of cumulative effects.

Landscape effects

7.14   The landscape impact assessment describes the likely nature and scale of changes to individual landscape elements and characteristics, and the consequential effect on the landscape character, resulting from the proposed development. When identifying and assessing landscape change, it is important to take into account the existing trends for change within the landscape, which may be due to natural processes or human activities.

The initial lists of likely effects, identified during the screening and scoping 7.15
stages, should be reviewed and amended to take into account the additional information obtained through consultation, baseline survey and development of the scheme design, including any integrated mitigation measures. Checklists and matrices can assist in this process where, for example, development features and construction activities are shown on one axis, with the potential landscape receptors on the other. (Examples of the potential sources of effects are identified in paragraph 7.5.)

Sensitivity of the landscape resource

The degree to which a particular landscape type or area can accommodate 7.16 change arising from a particular development, without detrimental effects on its character, will vary with:

- existing land use;

- the pattern and scale of the landscape;

- visual enclosure/openness of views, and distribution of visual receptors;

- the scope for mitigation, which would be in character with the existing landscape;

- the value placed on the landscape.

Variations of these characteristics within the local landscape and within the site need to be identified.

The determination of the sensitivity of the landscape resource is based upon an 7.17 evaluation of each key element or characteristic of the landscape likely to be affected. The evaluation will reflect such factors as its quality, value, contribution to landscape character, and the degree to which the particular element or characteristic can be replaced or substituted.

Scale or magnitude of landscape effects

In the evaluation of the effects it may be helpful to rank or quantify individual 7.18 effects within a series of levels or categories, indicating a gradation from high to low. Where used, a minimum of four levels or categories is recommended for both negative (adverse) and positive (beneficial) effects, as shown in Box 7.2. Different sets of criteria will be applicable to landscape and visual effects, but in all cases the criteria and thresholds should be clearly defined, simple, readily understood and applicable for all circumstances in which they are applied.

There is no standard methodology for the quantification of the scale or magni- 7.19 tude of relative effects. However, it is generally based on the scale or degree of change to the landscape resource, the nature of the effect and its duration

> ### Box 7.2 Example of levels or grades used in the evaluation of effect
>
> | Adverse | Beneficial |
> | --- | --- |
> | High/Substantial | High/Substantial |
> | Medium/Moderate | Medium/Moderate |
> | Low/Slight | Low/Slight |
> | No change | No change |
>
> (Examples of criteria used by practitioners are set out in Appendix 6)

including whether it is permanent or temporary. It may also be appropriate to consider whether the effects are reversible.

7.20   Some effects may be quantified, such as the number of mature trees and length of hedgerow to be lost as a result of the development. The details of any phasing, duration of the active operations (particularly relevant for landfill or mineral extraction development), and the extent of new and replacement planting to take place at restoration should also be described. This type of factual data is especially useful when comparing the effects at different stages of the project.

7.21   A distinction is made between the scale of the effect, the nature of the change and the duration, as follows:

- scale: large, medium, small, etc.;

- nature: negative (adverse) or positive (beneficial);

- duration: short, medium, long term/permanent or temporary.

7.22   Alternatively, the definitions and criteria for each level or scale or magnitude may combine the scale of the change in the landscape and its duration or degree of permanence. A judgement will need to be made about the weight to be given to each aspect in arriving at an overall value for scale or magnitude for each effect. The reasoning for these judgements should be recorded by description or in tabular form so that the assessment process is clearly set out and may be readily understood by the decision makers and members of the public.

7.23   More weight is usually given to effects that are greater in scale and permanent or long term. Therefore, a temporary change that is confined to a small area and visible only from a few private residential properties may be considered to be of low scale or magnitude. In assessing the duration of the effect, consideration should be given to the effectiveness of mitigation, particularly where planting is proposed for screening purposes. Where the planting may be out of character with its surroundings, this may increase the scale of the negative (adverse) changes to the landscape.

Visual effects

The assessment of visual effects describes: 7.24

- the changes in the character of the available views resulting from the development;

- the changes in the visual amenity of the visual receptors.

Identification of effects

The first task is the systematic identification of potential sources of effects with   7.25 respect to the potential visual receptors. As with landscape effects, checklists and matrices can often assist in this process. For example, a matrix showing different sources of visual change on one axis and the principal visual receptors affected on the other may assist in the initial identification of potential key effects for further study. The description of the effects should include cross references, if appropriate, to plans and other graphic material.

In the assessment of views there is likely to be a continuum in the degree of visi-   7.26 bility of the development from full view to no view. In order to assist in description and comparison of the effects on views, it may be helpful to use simplified categories which consider:

- the extent of the view that would be occupied by the development (degree of visual intrusion): full, partial, glimpse, etc.;

- the proportion of the development or particular features that would be visible: full, most, small amount, none;

- the distance of the viewpoint from the development and whether the viewpoint would focus on the development due to proximity or the development would form one element in a panoramic view;

- whether the view is transient or one of a sequence of views, as from a moving vehicle or footpath.

Changes in visual amenity may arise from both built or engineered forms and   7.27 soft landscape elements of the development. Consideration may also be given to the seasonal differences in effects arising from the degree of vegetative screening and/or filtering of views that will apply in summer and winter. Thus assessments may be provided for 'average' and 'worst-case' situations (the latter being the season with least leaf cover and therefore minimal vegetative screening).

7.28 People generally have differing responses to views and visual amenity depending on the context (location, time of day, degree of exposure) and purpose for being in a particular place (recreation, passing through a landscape, residence or employment, for example).

7.29 During passage through the landscape, certain activities or locations may be specifically associated with the experience and enjoyment of that landscape, such as the use of footpaths and tourist routes. It may therefore be appropriate in some circumstances to differentiate between the sensitivity of potential receptors for those using these routes as opposed to alternative routes.

7.30 Although residents may be particularly sensitive to changes in their visual amenity, most land use planning regimes consider that public views are of greater value than views from private property. However, the cumulative effects on a number of residents may be considered to give rise to an effect on the community. (See PPG 1 para 64). It is therefore important to assess all effects on public views and those from the curtilage of adjacent or nearby owners or occupiers within the same locality. (Note: when considering views from windows, views from rooms normally occupied during waking/daylight hours are generally deemed to be more important than those used for sleeping, from which only occasional views may be obtained.)

Sensitivity of visual receptors

7.31 The sensitivity of visual receptors and views will be dependent on:

- the location and context of the viewpoint;

- the expectations and occupation or activity of the receptor;

- the importance of the view (which may be determined with respect to its popularity or numbers of people affected, its appearance in guidebooks, on tourist maps, and in the facilities provided for its enjoyment and references to it in literature or art).

7.32 The most sensitive receptors may include:

- users of all outdoor recreational facilities including public rights of way, whose attention or interest may be focused on the landscape;

- communities where the development results in changes in the landscape setting or valued views enjoyed by the community;

- occupiers of residential properties with views affected by the development.

(See the guidance in the *Design Manual for Roads and Bridges* on scheduling properties and describing the effects in [16].)

Other receptors include:

- people engaged in outdoor sport or recreation (other than appreciation of the landscape, as in landscapes of acknowledged importance or value);

- people travelling through or past the affected landscape in cars, on trains or other transport routes;

- people at their place of work.

The least sensitive receptors are likely to be people at their place of work, or engaged 7.34
in similar activities, whose attention may be focused on their work or activity and who therefore may be potentially less susceptible to changes in the view.

In this process more weight is usually given to changes in the view or visual 7.35
amenity which are greater in scale, and visible over a wide area. In assessing the effect on views, consideration should be given to the effectiveness of mitigation measures, particularly where planting is proposed for screening purposes.

Scale or magnitude of visual effects

In the evaluation of the effects on views and the visual amenity of the identified 7.36
receptors, the magnitude or scale of visual change is described by reference to:

- the scale of change in the view with respect to the loss or addition of features in the view and changes in its composition including the proportion of the view occupied by the proposed development;

- the degree of contrast or integration of any new features or changes in the landscape with the existing or remaining landscape elements and characteristics in terms of form, scale and mass, line, height, colour and texture;

- the duration and nature of the effect, whether temporary or permanent, intermittent or continuous, etc.;

- the angle of view in relation to the main activity of the receptor;

- the distance of the viewpoint from the proposed development;

- the extent of the area over which the changes would be visible.

Numbers and types of viewers affected may be quantified where possible and 7.37
appropriate. These may also be indicated on plans with map symbols or tones used to denote the distribution of visual effects. The selection of viewpoints is important and normally reflects the principal representative viewpoints identified and, where possible, agreed with the regulatory authority during the baseline studies. The qualitative effects of the development on the character and quality of views requires careful consideration. Photomontages and other forms of visualisation can be useful supplements to the written description where appropriate.

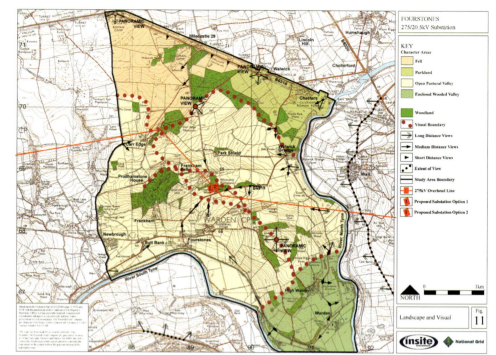

Significance of effects

7.38 Significance is not absolute and can only be defined in relation to each develop-ment and its location. It is for each assessment to determine the assessment criteria and the significance thresholds, using informed and well-reasoned judgement supported by thorough justification for their selection, and explana-tion as to how the conclusions about significance for each effect assessed have been derived.

7.39 The two principal criteria determining significance are the **scale** or **magnitude** of **effect** and the environmental **sensitivity of the location or receptor**. A higher level of significance is generally attached to large-scale effects and effects on sensitive or high-value receptors; thus small effects on highly sensitive sites can be more important than large effects on less sensitive sites. It is therefore important that a balanced and well-reasoned judgement of these two criteria is achieved.

7.40 For straightforward projects, separate assessments may be provided of the overall effect of the development proposal on the landscape as a whole and of the overall effect on visual amenity. More complex or very large projects and projects in environmentally sensitive locations require separate assessments of the effects of the different components of the development proposal, on each aspect of the landscape, i.e. landscape elements including special features and

---

Box 7.3   Determining the significance of environmental effects

The biggest challenge for all environmental professionals is assessing which impacts are significant and which are not. In England, a significant impact may be a material consideration for assessing the suitability of a planning application, but that is not how significance is defined in the Regulatory regime governing EIA, in part because it is set out in European legislation, where the English terminology is not used.

> Thus significance cannot be defined in any context independent of the proposal under consideration and its geographical context. That is, significance is unique for each proposal, although it is recognised that certain types of impact (for example, visually intrusive development [within or] adjacent to a National Park), might be generally considered significant.
>
> In North America, EA has been part of the Regulatory regime since 1969 under the National Environmental Policy Act (NEPA), which is under the control of the President's Council on Environmental Quality (CEQ). There, practitioners and the government agencies have accepted that significance is assessed on a case by case basis.

The significance of effects should be determined based on context and intensity (40CFR and 1508.27). Significance may vary with the setting of the proposed action:

> Thresholds and criteria (i.e., levels of acceptable change) used to determine the significance of effects will vary depending on the type of resource being analysed, the condition of the resource, the importance of the resource as an issue (as identified through scoping). Criteria can be quantitative units of measure such as those used to determine threshold values in economic impact modelling, or qualitative units of measure such as the perceptions of visitors to a recreational area. No matter how the criteria are derived, they should be directly related to the relevant cause-and-effect relationships. The criteria used, including quantitative thresholds if appropriate, should be clearly stated in the assessment document.
>
> (CEQ, January 1997)

---

characteristics of the resulting effect on landscape character. The visual assessment may similarly assess separately the effects on individual views and on visual amenity for the individual receptors.

The aim of this approach is to increase the transparency of the assessment process and provide the relevant information to the decision makers in a useful format. Separation into components will also help to reveal conflicts between them – for example, a scheme may have a beneficial effect on biodiversity (by   7.41

habitat creation through new woodlands and ponds) but it may also have an adverse effect on landscape character and visual amenity if the new habitats are not appropriate to their setting.

7.42 In the context of EIA, 'significance' varies with the type of project and the topic under assessment. For some topics such as noise, air and water quality, levels of magnitude or scale will be based on established, measurable technical thresholds, and the sensitivity of receptors may also be defined in statutory regulations or planning guidance. No such formal guidance exists for the assessment of significance for landscape and visual effects and the assessor must clearly define the criteria used in the assessment for each project, using his or her skill based on professional judgement. The important objective is to identify to whom and to what degree an effect is significant. It may be helpful to define levels or categories of significance (including 'not significant') appropriate to the nature, size and location of the proposed development. Within the framework of an EIA, the levels of significance may need to be consistent with the overall approach applied to the other topics.

Significance of landscape effects

7.43 In establishing a judgement concerning the significance of landscape effects, the following general guidance should be noted:

- The loss of mature or diverse landscape elements, or features, is likely to be more significant than the loss of new or uniform/homogenous elements.

- Effects on character areas, which are distinctive or representative, may be more important than the loss of areas in poor condition or degraded character which may, however, present greater opportunities for enhancement.

- The loss of landscape elements, features or characteristics will be given greater weight if they are identified as being of high value or importance. Thus, effects on landscape areas or characteristics recognised for their national importance are likely to be of more significance than effects on areas or characteristics of local importance. The test is whether the integrity of the landscape and objectives of designation are compromised or not.

- The sensitivity of the landscape is dependent on both the attributes of the receiving environment and the characteristics and effects of the proposed development and can only be established by carrying out the assessment. However, landscapes with a high value and sensitivity to the type of change proposed are likely to be more seriously affected by development than those with a lower sensitivity.

- The test of significance is not directly related to planning policy. However, this may be an important consideration where policies identify commonly held objectives and values.

An approach in which landscape effects are assessed in relation to individual components of the landscape provides a clearer analysis of the effects of the proposals. It can also highlight differences between the sensitivity of the landscape (its ability to accommodate change caused by a particular development without adverse effects on its character) and landscape value/importance. The balance between these two aspects needs to be carefully considered. The methodology adopted should make it clear how the different issues have been assessed and what weight has been given to each in determining the overall significance.

It will be evident that the analysis of criteria involves considerable judgement in 7.45 balancing the complex relationships between the different components of the landscape. The critical part of this process is to explain how the assessment has been built up, and how the criteria have been selected and applied. This is particularly important at the final assessment stage, where a further judgement has to be undertaken in order to identify the significant effects and, if required, their degree of significance.

The results of the analysis may be presented in a table or schedule, which 7.46 summarises the information on which the assessment is based and concludes with a statement of significance. Further detailed information can be provided in the text if required, including an indication of how the opinions of others have been taken into account. This may be particularly relevant where there is a difference of opinion, when it may be helpful to explain why these differences have arisen.

The relationship between the sensitivity of the receptor and the nature and scale 7.47 or magnitude of the effect is sometimes presented in the form of a simple matrix. However in such a matrix the relationship between the two axes is not linear. The axes are also likely to have different weightings, as the nature and scale of effects are largely derived from objective data, while the sensitivity and value of a landscape resource is largely derived from subjective judgements.

Significance of effects on visual amenity

As for landscape effects, the significance of visual effects will be assessed by 7.48 taking into consideration the sensitivity and importance of the receptor and the nature, scale or magnitude and duration of the change or effect.

In establishing a judgement concerning significance of visual effects, the 7.49 following general guidance should be noted:

- Large-scale changes which introduce new, discordant or intrusive elements into the view are more likely to be significant than small changes or changes involving features already present within the view.

- Changes in views from recognised and important viewpoints or amenity routes are likely to be more significant than changes affecting other less important paths and roads.

- Changes affecting large numbers of people are generally more significant than those affecting a relatively small group of users. However, in wilderness landscapes the sensitivity of the people who use these areas may be very high and this will be reflected in the significance of the change.

7.50   The results of a visual analysis may be usefully summarised in table form, setting out the numbers of receptors (properties, roads, paths, etc.), importance of the view, sensitivity of the receptors, magnitude of effect and the overall assessment of significance.

7.51   The examples given in Appendix 6 present different approaches to specific situations. The individual carrying out landscape and visual impact assessments should use a method and criteria that is appropriate to their assessment. It should also be remembered that the assessment is not required to describe every effect of the proposed development, only the main or likely significant effects on the environment which are required to inform the decision-making authority, in their determination of the planning application. (See Part 9 for further information on consultation.)

Part 8

Presentation techniques
Good practice

Introduction

This section provides information on presentation techniques that may be used 8.1
to communicate the results of landscape and visual assessments, whether
free-standing or as part of an EIA. In all cases the appropriate techniques must be
carefully chosen and rigorously applied, as they will be subject to close scrutiny
and, in the case of contentious developments, they may need to be explained
and substantiated at a Public Inquiry.

Presentation of findings

The precise content of a landscape and visual impact assessment may vary 8.2
considerably, depending on factors such as the scope of work agreed with the
regulatory authority and consultees and the sensitivity of the affected landscape
and visual resources.

The general opening sections of the landscape and visual impact assessment 8.3
present basic information on the objectives, responsibilities and methodology,
and may include:

- the planning and legal context, including published policies and guidance
  on landscape designations and landscape character areas in the vicinity of
  the development;

- the remit, qualifications and experience of those responsible for preparing
  the assessment;

- the methodology used, including the overall assessment process, the link to
  scheme design, and the specific techniques used at each stage in the assessment;

- the scope of the assessment, key issues, how these were determined and any
  constraints or data deficiencies that may apply.

Text should be concise, to the point and impartial, with definitions provided for 8.4
any technical terms that are used, supported by the glossary of terms. The assessments should include:

- a clear description of the basic elements of the development of relevance to
  the landscape and visual assessments;

- an understanding of landscape constraints and opportunities;

- a systematic identification and evaluation of potential effects;

- a sound prediction of the magnitude of effects;

- reasoned criteria and judgements for evaluating the significance of effects;

- measures to address adverse effects.

8.5 Landscape and visual impact assessments are not usually carried out in isolation but generally form part of a wider assessment of environmental impact that may arise from a proposed development. Nevertheless, the report resulting from the landscape and visual impact assessments can be presented as a 'stand-alone' document. The information may be integrated into a formal Environmental Statement, or where a formal EIA is not required, it may be used as a supplementary report to accompany a planning application.

8.6 The preparation of a non-technical summary (NTS) of the Environmental Statement is a formal requirement, and is expressly intended to help the general public and interested parties to participate in the decision-making process from an informed position. The NTS is normally illustrated with photographs and easily understood plans. Summary descriptions are cross-referenced back to the full ES, so that the reader can refer to it for more detail if required.

8.7 **Illustrations** communicate information more quickly and easily than text. They have a more important role in relation to landscape and visual effects than any other topics, as much landscape and visual information is best communicated through maps, plans, photographs and other illustrative media. The choice of scale and presentational techniques is crucial, with illustrations limited to information of specific relevance to the assessment. The inclusion of detailed design and technical drawings is generally not appropriate. Illustrations should be closely linked to the text, complementing rather than duplicating its content. It is important to illustrate how the development will relate to both the human scale and the scale of the surrounding landscape.

8.8 **Photographs** have a special role in the description of landscape character and key views, but need to be impartial and objective to avoid misleading impressions. The choice of viewpoints should be justified, and the location and precise direction of view shown on an accompanying map. Seasonal and atmospheric effects and lens type and focal length are also stated, together with reasons for the choice of lens.

8.9 **Charts and tables** can be effective, providing a useful summary of data. In particular they can permit ready comparison, between different scheme options and types of effect, which can be valuable, especially in the early stages of planning and design. In addition, they are probably the best way of making complex information more accessible to consultees and the public. Preparation must be careful and consistent, as they may be relied upon by decision makers.

Step 1   Discuss the project with the client to establish the precise objective. Assess the type of graphics and presentation likely to be most appropriate for the proposed development. There is little advantage in using advanced techniques if a simple thumbnail sketch may be more appropriate.

Step 2   Explore the further scope of the project to determine other options available to the client from two-dimensional photomontages to three-dimensional animation or fully interactive virtual reality.

Step 3   For any given project, be precise about the level of costs associated with each presentation style to enable the client to make an informed choice – a cost–benefit analysis chart may be prepared for each technique.

Step 4   Identify delivery dates for the presentation material and chart this back from critical milestones such as a submission for planning, to ensure an appropriate lead-in time is allowed for delivery of Ordnance Survey data or preparation of a site survey.

Step 5   Agree with the client the technique to be used, projected costs and a programme.

Step 6   Allow time for consultation with the client at an intermediate stage to permit slight changes in the direction or emphasis of the project.

Figure 8.1   Choosing the right illustrative technique

Figure 8.1 provides a framework for identifying appropriate techniques with a client, which include a selection of computer graphics applications that can be tailored to make presentations more informative and cost effective. Attention is also drawn to the detailed advice on the use of computer presentation techniques, including visual envelope maps, in Appendix 8.   8.10

Visibility mapping

Visibility mapping and visualisation techniques are central to the effective prediction and communication of landscape and visual effects. The following comprises a brief synopsis of common techniques, but reference may also be made to the more detailed guidance in Appendix 9.   8.11

A visibility map can indicate the visibility of the site (the baseline conditions), or the proposed development within it. Both may be relevant, as the existing visibility of the site may contribute to the visual amenity of the surrounding area. In addition, for complex developments, it may be appropriate to indicate separately the areas from which the whole development will be visible, or one part of the development such as the top of a tall structure, such as the turbines from a wind farm.   8.12

8.13 Manual estimation of visibility from topographic maps is possible, but computer mapping of visibility is particularly helpful for large-scale or complex developments. However, when using a bare ground ZVI to measure the extent of visibility, its application can be limited, particularly in a flat landscape where visibility is determined by land use rather than topographic features. For distant views, an allowance should be considered for the curvature of the earth's surface and refraction effects of the earth's atmosphere.

8.14 It is essential for visibility to be checked and confirmed in the field because of the localised screening effects of built elements, minor landform features and vegetation. Summer and winter effects may also need to be examined separately to ensure that the limited screening effect of deciduous winter vegetation is taken into account. Accurate estimation of the visibility of proposed tall structures can pose particular problems. Although there are ways of dealing with this, such as flying a balloon and using scaffolds and cranes to act as a reference point at the same height and location as the proposed structure, the practicality of such measures must obviously be taken into account. It is generally simpler and more accurate to input the heights of proposed structures, tall buildings, plantations, etc. into a three-dimensional computer model where alternative height options may be also examined more readily.

Visualisations

8.15 Since the first guidelines were produced in 1995, the quality of presentation techniques and technical drawing using computer-aided drafting has advanced substantially. There is, however, a responsibility to make a discerning use of technology – in some instances blending traditional techniques with the new – to ensure that the choice of graphic technique is determined by the need to communicate the required information in the most accurate way.

8.16 Visualisations are one of the best means of communicating the landscape and visual effects of a development to decision makers and the public, but accuracy is essential. Viewpoints should be selected with respect to the location, season and timing relative to a project's life cycle and include conditions indicating the worst-case situation.

8.17 A growing range of visualisation techniques is available, and computer technology and multimedia now present significant opportunities for landscape and environmental professionals engaged in all aspects of EIA, planning and design work. At the upper end of the range are three-dimensional computer simulations, such as virtual reality models built up from Ordnance Survey, digital terrain maps and data from aerial photography, drawing on a sufficiently wide area to demonstrate the context of a proposed development. Once the three-dimensional model has been created, it becomes possible to view any aspect of a development from any viewpoint contained within the boundary of the model. These techniques have great potential, especially in relation to linear developments such as roads and transmission lines, as once baseline conditions are modelled, variations to a scheme can be relatively easily produced and compared.

The precise choice of technique for a particular scheme will depend on the nature of the development, data available, timing and budget. A number of methods for creating a variety of presentation techniques are considered below.   8.18

Photomontages

A photomontage is the superimposition of an image onto a photograph for the purpose of creating a realistic representation of proposed or potential changes to any view. Traditionally, these were created manually by hand rendering. Today most are generated using computer imagery.   8.19

Photomontages are a popular visualisation technique. Their main advantage is that they can illustrate the development within the 'real' landscape and from known viewpoints. Technically-accurate photomontages may require specialist advice. This requires the precise locations and dimensions of the development, for other features forming reference points in the view, the accurate location and height from which the photograph was taken, and focal length and precise direction of view of the camera, to correctly place the development within the photograph. A computer-generated perspective of key structures will also be required for built developments. Technical accuracy and skill are needed to alter photographs to realistically illustrate the new buildings, ground form and planting within the photographic view (see Appendix 7 for additional information).   8.20

Other visualisation techniques may be appropriate under certain circumstances, including overlays; perspective sketches, which may be constructed over computer-generated wire lines; physical models, which tend to be expensive but can be useful in public consultations; and video simulations, which can show movement, for example, of wind turbines. Photographs of similar projects can also be helpful, provided it is made clear that they are indicative only. Artist's impressions that are not accurately constructed are not recommended.   8.21

Case study

Glebe Farm
Wavendon, Buckinghamshire

October 2000
Client: Gallagher Estates Ltd/
Wilcon Homes Ltd
Principal author: Terence O'Rourke plc

CONTEXT

Urban/urban fringe   Site south east of Milton Keynes' urban centre close to Wavendon village and adjacent to a principal entrance road to the city from M1

Rural   Land contributes to village setting and immediate landscape character. However, adjacent employment allocations in local plan for Milton Keynes' eastern expansion may alter perception

Illustrative perspective sketch

DETAILS OF PROPOSAL

Summary description	Evolution of sketch proposals for mixed use development maximising location proximity to local facilities and catering for future highway growth. Presentation of a distinctive development character based on a network of streets within a landscape framework, generating variety of form/texture.
Nature and scope of issues	Relationship to nearby development; public/pedestrian links. Visual/acoustic/aesthetic consideration of proximity to road development. Site drainage considerations and visual assimilation into the landform. Scale and form in relation to village setting and sustainability of proposals.
Planning/ regulatory content	Promotion of the site through the local plan process. Sensitive location adjacent to a Conservation Area.

CASE ANALYSIS

Approach	Understanding the receiving and future landscape using site appraisal and development studies was fundamental in shaping proposals. Public views were also critical. The aim was to promote a distinctive development character with a strong visual identity. The landscape framework provides functional opportunities for accommodation and mitigation works, bringing significant ecological and visual benefits.
Methodology	CCP423, CCP326 and GLVIA.
Application of methodology	Detailed site appraisal.

Presentation	Aerial photographs, artists impressions, plan and map-based information to promote development concepts/form, demonstrating evolution of proposals.

Sketch illustrative layout

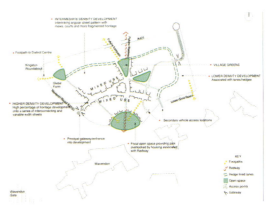

Issues and opportunities

Additional facility provision

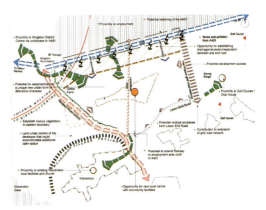

Proposals concept – central form

Development forms

CRITIQUE/CONCLUSIONS

Critique	A combination of detailed computer-drawn sketch plans identifies the significant issues and opportunities illustrating a clear and simplified approach to site planning and resultant proposals within a very 'user-friendly' document.
	This approach allowed the complex issues to be clearly conveyed.

Case study

<table>
<tr>
<td>

Sandown Wastewater Treatment Works
Sandown, Isle of Wight

1996–2000
Client: Southern Water Services Ltd
Principal author: Terence O'Rourke

</td>
</tr>
</table>

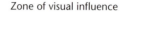

Zone of visual influence

<table>
<tr>
<td>

CONTEXT

Urban/urban fringe   Located within the coastal plain adjacent to the northern boundary of Sandown

Rural   Lies adjacent to the Sandown Levels and bordered by the Eastern Yar River

</td>
</tr>
</table>

DETAILS OF PROPOSAL

Summary description	Proposals for the development of major new wastewater treatment and recycling plant to serve the Isle of Wight on and adjacent to existing treatment works. Development included extensive temporary construction of pipelines, outfalls, and construction yards. Initial proposals for primary treatment expanded to include dryer building and secondary treatment facilities.
Nature and scope of issues	Sensitive location in generally flat coastal landscape visible from attractive high land to the north/north west. Overlooked by downland with prime coastal view. Extensive potential visibility from adjacent coastal/residential locations; within clear site of extensive AONB chalk downland. Scale of buildings and extent of development on constrained site. Portion of site composed of contaminated land requiring amelioration. Site not identified for expansion; promoted through application and ES.

CASE ANALYSIS

Approach	Extensive land appraisal resulting in detailed understanding of site, setting, character and visibility; also the nature and extent of proposals and potential effects in relation to carefully identified viewpoints. Identification of the resulting key landscape issues with extent and significance of predicted landscape change. Mitigation strategy resulted in development of visual principles to guide building form and location.
Application of methodology	Desktop studies and research; extensive fieldwork; photographs – both 35mm for presentation and 210 zoom for accuracy and definition; visual envelopes; ZVI; photograph annotation; mitigation strategies; 3D computer modelling; and computer prediction of views to understand visual significance of layout.
Presentation	Presentation included sketches, diagrams, drawings and computer-generated 3D models and elevations.

Isometric views and
elevations of 3D model

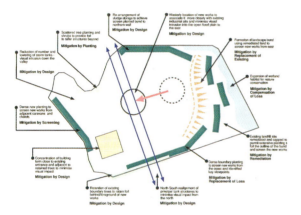

Landscape mitigation measures

CRITIQUE/CONCLUSIONS

Critique	A comprehensive understanding of the site and setting and clear identification of receptors enabled the final proposals to minimise the visual profile of the proposal from principal viewpoints. Principles such as tank alignments, building location and built profile evolved from identified mitigation measures.
Conclusion	This process ensured subsequent development changes were considered against established principles and tested by computer modelling. This ability to model the predicted view of the final proposals enabled the relocation of structures within the site to ensure impact was minimised from key locations.
Cumulative effects	The resulting constructed proposals clearly demonstrate the effectiveness of the adopted techniques in enabling accommodation of a significant development of large-scale buildings and structures within a relatively confined and contaminated site in a sensitive location visible from an AONB.

Digital plans and masterplans

8.22   CAD also facilitates the production of composite plans from multiple layers of different types of information. Thus any combination of information 'layers' such as drainage, ecology, landscape assessment, etc. may be brought together to enable ready comparison of data and enable special interests to inform the design process.

8.23   To complement technical plans in CAD, computer graphics now also play an increased role in the preparation of presentation plans. In particular, elaborate masterplans can be rendered in the computer using scanned or hand-drawn textures to create realistic 'aerial view' impressions.

8.24   Digitally-rendered plans are more flexible than traditional hand-rendered drawings in a number of areas. As a digitally coloured masterplan is developed, multiple copies may be run off rapidly and inexpensively at various sizes for discussion. Similarly, a series of alternative plans can be readily produced from the original base to illustrate the development and associated landscape proposals through time. Revisions and amendments to a part or parts of the proposal can be carried out much more easily than an art medium would permit, and the final drawing can be reproduced in colour at a variety of scales with little apparent reduction in quality. Alternatively, it may be supplied as a CD-Rom or incorporated in a presentation software program such as Powerpoint, distributed over the Internet or made available on web sites.

Part 9

Consultation and review

Consultation and the assessment process

Consultation is an essential part of the landscape and visual impact assessment process, whether for the purpose of gathering specific information about the site, or for canvassing the views of the public on the proposed development. It can be a valuable tool in seeking understanding and agreement about key issues and can highlight local interests and values, which may otherwise be overlooked. With commitment and engagement in a genuinely open and responsive process, consultation can also make a real contribution to scheme design.

9.1

Consultation may take a variety of forms and fulfil many purposes at different stages in the assessment. It offers the opportunity to gain advice and help from a wide range of organisations, individuals, local communities and interest groups on a formal and informal basis. It may involve the regulatory authority, statutory consultees, amenity and conservation bodies and local residents. Without effective consultation, the assessment process as a whole may be diminished.

9.2

In the initial stages of project planning, consultation with the regulatory authority aims to establish the likely acceptability of the proposed development, and the preferred development site. When an EIA is required, or when an applicant advises the regulatory authority of the decision to prepare an ES voluntarily, the regulatory authority will inform the statutory consultees. This places them under an obligation to provide, on request, information that is likely to be relevant to the assessment, such as previous landscape surveys or assessments of the area, and advice on the basis for landscape and other designations. The aim of consultations with the regulatory authority and other statutory consultees is to arrive at consensus on matters such as terms of reference, methodology and assessment techniques.

9.3

The interim presentation of information about the project to interested parties can help to maintain goodwill, especially where a two-way exchange of ideas and views on scheme design can be initiated. The timing of involvement will depend upon many factors, including the nature of the development, but generally the earlier the better. Such participation may not always result in full agreement, but it may serve to resolve some issues and to clarify any remaining objections. In its most useful form, participation in consultation will improve the quality of the information influencing the scheme design, and may result in positive changes to the design. Later in the assessment process, consultation will be more concerned with information dissemination, particularly to the regulatory authority and statutory consultees.

9.4

Guidelines for consultation

9.5   The views of the regulatory authority, or consultees, are not necessarily representative of the views of local people, which may be sought directly, through exhibitions, meetings, questionnaires or by other means. This form of consultation can
provide an opportunity to set out clearly the issues involved in the proposed
development and to draw out local concern, and identify the aspects of the
proposal that are important in local opinion.

9.6   The particular agenda and terms of reference of any organisation consulted is
taken into account when assessing the weight to be given to their views, and
how they may influence the project proposals. While important, such views will
need to be weighed in the balance with many other factors, such as government
policy, or the provisions of the development plan. For both statutory and
non-statutory consultees it is important to distinguish between 'in principle'
objections (which may colour their judgement) and specific comments on the
proposals.

9.7   Consultation can be a difficult process. The developer may be reluctant to release
information about the development for reasons of commercial sensitivity or
uncertainty. There may also be a perception that to invite discussion and debate
is to subject the project to 'unnecessary' interference. Statutory consultees and
members of the public may be suspicious about the consultation process and
could be uncompromisingly hostile to the proposed development. They may
also be concerned that they will prejudice their future position, by becoming too
closely involved and may need to be persuaded that the offer to participate is
genuine. In such circumstances, a poorly-managed programme of consultations
could generate adverse publicity.

9.8   Most of these reservations can be overcome if the consultation programme is
guided by the following principles:

- Consultation must be **genuine and open**. The temptation to make the
most of consultation for information gathering, while being reluctant to
disseminate information, is to be resisted.

- The **timing of consultation** should be **carefully planned** to prevent
premature disclosure, which might encourage blight or make developers
commercially vulnerable. There may be occasions where controlled release
of information or confidentiality safeguards are required.

- Requests for **participation** should be **timely**. There is no point in
seeking ideas and views if it is actually too late for the scheme design to be
modified. Sufficient time must also be allowed for consultees to be able to
consider and act on the information provided.

- The **objectives of consultation** should be **clearly stated**. Information presented to consultees should be appropriate in content and level of detail, clearly identifying those issues on which comment is being sought.

Consultation methods

The objectives for consultation and the stage in the assessment process will dictate the method or combination of methods used for consultation, but informal and early consultations have the greatest potential for success. The main consultation methods that can be used are described below. Public consultation methodology is an expanding area, and new techniques such as referenda, local juries and the Internet are being introduced. The following techniques represent those in current widespread use. As other techniques emerge, the landscape professional should ensure that the most appropriate consultation method is adopted for the particular circumstances of the project and consultees. 9.9

Correspondence

This is used for information gathering and dissemination, inviting comment and recording issues that have been discussed and agreed. 9.10

Face-to-face discussion

Direct discussion with relevant parties, particularly the planning or regulatory authority, conservation agencies and other statutory or informal consultees is an important element of consultation. For some developments, a liaison or advisory group may also be cost effective, make the consultation process less time consuming, and assist in achieving a consensus view. Early joint site visits could be helpful in exploring landscape opportunities and constraints. 9.11

Presentations and informal public meetings

Selective presentations, such as those to local council members may be useful, but can alienate excluded parties. Open public meetings may facilitate public participation, but can be difficult to record and manage in order to avoid fruitless confrontation between objectors and the developers. 9.12

Exhibitions

Exhibitions can present a great deal of information to a broad range of parties including the general public. They present an opportunity for friendly and constructive exchange of views between the design or assessment team and members of the public who may be directly affected by the proposals. Feedback from public consultations should be produced in a suitable form for analysis, which can then be taken into account in the development of the project proposals. 9.13

Workshops

9.14   Workshops are highly structured, sometimes public, meetings, in which those attending are expected to participate and produce results, which can be fed into the decision-making process. They can be particularly useful for examining options for impact mitigation. Workshop participants may be selected as representative of particular interest groups or as a cross section of interests. To be effective participants should be limited to a maximum of twenty, with five to six for intensive 'brain-storming' on particular topics.

Leaflets and mailings

9.15   Lastly, consultation material may also be presented to the public through leaflets or mailings to representative groups or to all affected local residents. This approach is often used in conjunction with public exhibitions, and may include a questionnaire to allow written responses to be gathered. In relation to landscape and visual impacts, views can be sought on preferred landscape enhancement measures and on the form of mitigation that would meet local needs and support.

9.16   Whatever method of consultation is chosen, a means of recording response is essential to ensure the exercise is meaningful and fruitful. The methodology must be clearly explained when reporting the results.

9.17   The non-technical summary can also be useful in public consultation, if it is available, particularly as it is prepared with the lay audience specifically in mind.

9.18   A balanced assessment of the views of consultees may be presented as a separate section of the EIA, explaining whether and how these views have been taken into account. Where there is a difference between professional judgement and the views of consultees or the public, it is helpful to suggest the possible reasons for the differences.

The role of the regulatory authority

How the authority can help

9.19   The principal issues for the regulatory authority, and those statutory consultees who have a strong interest in the landscape, are:

- how to encourage the best result from the developer;

- the adequacy of the landscape and visual components of an ES;

- successful implementation and monitoring of scheme proposals.

With appropriate professional expertise, the regulatory authority's role in guiding the developer will serve the interests of the general public and of the authority itself, as well as those of the developer. It will also ensure that the scope of the ES submitted is adequate, that the appropriate degree of consideration has been given to the factors affecting the landscape and visual amenity, and will enable the authority to assess the quality of the ES.

Guidance to the developer

Regulatory authorities can give support and guidance to those responsible for the planning, design and assessment of new developments, in accordance with their own policies, interests and objectives. The developer may rely on information or opinions provided by the authority over a long period of time. It is therefore important that the advice is consistent and reflects the authority's position (rather than the views of individual officers). The authority may provide guidance on the landscape planning context, the scope and content of an ES, and the authority's expectations for the landscape design proposals. 9.21

Landscape context and design principles

The general planning context for new development is contained in statutes and regulations, in government guidance, and in formal development plan policies, which indicate in broad terms what types of development will be acceptable in what locations. Regulatory authorities can also make a positive contribution to the development process in producing development briefs for specific sites. 9.22

Area-wide landscape character assessments and strategies may provide a clear framework for the consideration of landscape issues in development control, and an indication of the preferred or most suitable areas for particular developments. They can also provide useful information on landscape character; areas identified for landscape conservation, restoration or reconstruction; and on issues such as urban fringe landscape degradation or industrial dereliction. At a more detailed level, landscape design guidance can indicate preferred materials, and choice of plant species. 9.23

Content of the landscape and visual impact assessment

The regulatory authority may be expected to work closely with the developer on the terms of reference, scope and methodology for the landscape and visual impact assessment. The authority is required to comment on the specific content of the ES and the level of detail that they consider would be appropriate to the assessment. They may also be a source of useful information, including: 9.24

- checklists of information held by the authority, and additional baseline survey information as available;

- advice on environmental constraints including landscape designations;

- general principles and objectives regarding landscape enhancement and mitigation measures.

9.25 This advice can be helpful to developers, especially at an early stage in the assessment process, but it is no substitute for a comprehensive landscape and visual impact assessment. It may also be helpful for the authority to review and agree baseline survey findings, criteria and thresholds for the assessment of effects, and 'performance standards' for mitigation of key impacts.

9.26 The future management and maintenance of a landscape scheme or restoration proposals may be agreed with the regulatory authority and embodied in the submitted proposals and ES. Similarly, the authority may wish to agree in advance appropriate planning conditions, subject to an approval, to ensure implementation of the landscape proposals, or in the case of minerals and waste disposal sites, phased programmes of working and restoration, or monitoring mechanisms.

Review of the landscape and visual impact assessment

9.27 The regulatory authority has a key role in the collation and consideration of relevant comments from statutory consultees and reviewing the adequacy of the landscape and visual impact assessment. The review process will check that the assessment meets the requirements of the EIA regulations and also the specific terms of reference discussed and agreed with the developer, during scoping or subsequent consultations. The authority may consider whether it would be advisable to seek specialist advice or expertise, or indeed to appoint an independent third party as assessor. Whichever approach is used, the review should consider:

- the scope and content of baseline studies;

- the methodology and techniques applied; accuracy and completeness of identification and evaluation of potential effects;

- the criteria and thresholds used to assess the effects predicted;

- the effectiveness of proposed mitigation, and success in communicating results.

9.28 The IEMA has developed a set of general criteria for reviewing ESs that can also be applied to the landscape and visual impact assessment section of the ES. In addition, the University of Manchester, in work published by the Countryside Agency and endorsed by the Countryside Council for Wales, has developed specific criteria for review of landscape impact assessments.

Implementation and monitoring

The granting of development consent is not the end of the process. The developer 9.29
and the regulatory authority have a responsibility to ensure that commitments
made in the application and the ES are honoured during construction, operation, subsequent site management and restoration. Usually implementation is
achieved through the enforcement of consent conditions, legal agreements,
undertakings or other requirements.

To be effective, these conditions and requirements must be relevant, fair, reason- 9.30
able and enforceable. They can be based in part on standard landscape conditions, such as those provided in government guidance, tailored to reflect the
particular needs of the scheme concerned. The most important undertakings for
highways development are likely to relate to ground modelling and screen
planting while planning conditions for mineral extraction schemes will focus on
phased working, progressive restoration and aftercare of restored areas. Where
the effectiveness of proposed mitigation measures is uncertain, performance
standards may be applied, and appropriate monitoring procedures incorporated
in the implementation process. Non-compliance with planning conditions can
lead to statutory enforcement proceedings. In certain cases a financial bond or
legal agreement attached to the planning consent may be appropriate, to ensure
mitigation measures are successfully completed.

Mitigation measures may require long-term management and monitoring. 9.31
Monitoring can fulfil a number of very useful purposes including:

- establishing whether or not predicted impacts have actually occurred;

- identifying unforeseen impacts and omissions from the original ES and
  ensuring an appropriate response;

- checking compliance with proposed mitigation measures and planning
  conditions;

- checking the effectiveness of mitigation measures in avoiding or reducing
  adverse impacts.

There are many advantages to be gained from monitoring impacts and mitiga- 9.32
tion in this way. With appropriate feedback to similar future assessments, the
quality of impact prediction can be improved through time. Remedial action can
sometimes be taken to address unforeseen impacts and enforcement action
carried out where necessary to ensure that the mitigation measures that were
promised are implemented, and are effective. The development of explicit monitoring programmes for landscape and visual impacts is therefore strongly
encouraged.

9.33 The responsibility for monitoring lies jointly with the developer and the regulatory authority. For the developer, monitoring can enhance credibility and public confidence, as well as ensuring the successful outcome of the project. For the regulatory authority, monitoring offers the opportunity to check on the effectiveness of mitigation and take appropriate action to ensure that landscape conservation and enhancement objectives have in fact been achieved. Finally, monitoring can also help to improve the future practice of landscape and visual impact assessment, by providing feedback on the accuracy of assessment techniques.

Glossary

Analysis (landscape)   The process of breaking the landscape down into its component parts to understand how it is made up.

Assessment (landscape)   An umbrella term for description, classification and analysis of landscape.

Biodiversity   The concept of variety in all species of plants and animals through which nature finds its balance.

Classification   A process of sorting the landscape into different types using selected criteria but without attaching relative values to the different kinds of landscape.

Compensation   The measures taken to offset or compensate for residual adverse effects that cannot be mitigated, or for which mitigation cannot entirely eliminate adverse effects.

Constraints map   Map showing the location of important resources and receptors that may form constraints to development.

Countryside   The rural environment and its associated communities (including the coast).

Cumulative effects   The summation of effects that result from changes caused by a development in conjunction with other past, present or reasonably foreseeable actions.

Diversity   Where a variety of qualities or characteristics occurs.

'Do nothing' situation   Continued change/evolution of landscape or of the environment in the absence of the proposed development.

Element   A component part of the landscape (for example, roads, hedges, woods).

Enhancement   Landscape improvement through restoration, reconstruction or creation.

Environment   Our physical surroundings including air, water and land.

Environmental appraisal   A generic term for the evaluation of the environmental implications of proposals (used by the UK Government in respect of policies and plans).

Environmental fit   The relationship of a development to identified environmental opportunities and constraints in its setting.

Environmental Impact Assessment   The evaluation of the effects on the environment of particular development proposals.

Field pattern   The pattern of hedges and walls that define fields in farmed landscapes.

Geographical Information System   Computerised database of geographical information that can easily be updated and manipulated.

Heritage   Historic or cultural associations.

Indirect impacts   Impacts on the environment, which are not a direct result of the development but are often produced away from it or as a result of a complex pathway. Sometimes referred to as secondary impacts.

Landcover   Combinations of land use and vegetation that cover the land surface.

Landform   Combinations of slope and elevation that produce the shape and form of the land.

Landscape   Human perception of the land conditioned by knowledge and identity with a place.

Landscape capacity   The degree to which a particular landscape character type or area is able to accommodate change without unacceptable adverse effects on its character. Capacity is likely to vary according to the type and nature of change being proposed.

Landscape character   The distinct and recognisable pattern of elements that occurs consistently in a particular type of landscape, and how this is perceived by people. It reflects particular combinations of geology, landform, soils, vegetation, land use and human settlement. It creates the particular sense of place of different areas of the landscape.

Landscape character type   A landscape type will have broadly similar patterns of geology, landform, soils, vegetation, land use, settlement and field pattern discernible in maps and field survey records.

Landscape effects   Change in the elements, characteristics, character and qualities of the landscape as a result of development. These effects can be positive or negative.

Landscape evaluation   The process of attaching value (non-monetary) to a particular landscape, usually by the application of previously agreed criteria, including consultation and third party documents, for a particular purpose (for example, designation or in the context of the assessment).

Landscape factor   A circumstance or influence contributing to the impression of a landscape (for example, scale, enclosure, elevation).

Landscape feature   A prominent eye-catching element, for example, wooded hilltop or church spire.

Landscape quality (or condition)   is based on judgements about the physical state of the landscape, and about its intactness, from visual, functional, and ecological perspectives. It also reflects the state of repair of individual features and elements which make up the character in any one place.

Landscape resource   The combination of elements that contribute to landscape context, character and value.

Landscape sensitivity   The extent to which a landscape can accept change of a particular type and scale without unacceptable adverse effects on its character.

Land use   The primary use of the land, including both rural and urban activities.

Landscape value   The relative value or importance attached to a landscape (often as a basis for designation or recognition), which expresses national or local consensus, because of its quality, special qualities including perceptual aspects such as scenic beauty, tranquillity or wildness, cultural associations or other conservation issues.

Magnitude   A combination of the scale, extent and duration of an effect.

Methodology   The specific approach and techniques used for a given study.

Mitigation   Measures, including any process, activity or design to avoid, reduce, remedy or compensate for adverse landscape and visual effects of a development project.

Perception (of landscape)   The psychology of seeing and possibly attaching value and/or meaning (to landscape).

Precautionary principle   Principle applied to err on the side of caution where significant environmental damage may occur, but where knowledge on the matter is incomplete, or when the prediction of environmental effects is uncertain.

Preference   The liking by people for one particular landscape element, characteristic or feature over another.

Quality   See **landscape quality**.

Receptor   Physical landscape resource, special interest or viewer group that will experience an effect.

Regulatory authority   The planning or other authority responsible for planning consents or project authorisation (synonymous with determining authority or competent authority).

Scenario   A picture of a possible future.

Scoping   The process of identifying the likely significant effects of a development on the environment.

Sense of place (*genius loci*)   The essential character and spirit of an area: *genius loci* literally means 'spirit of the place'.

Sensitive/sensitivity   See **landscape sensitivity**.

Sieve mapping   Technique for mapping environmental constraints, working from a series of overlays, sieving out less important factors.

Sustainability   The principle that the environment should be protected in such a condition and to such a degree that ensures new development meets the needs of the present without compromising the ability of future generations to meet their own needs.

Technique   Specific working process.

Threshold   A specified level in grading effects, for example, of magnitude, sensitivity or significance.

Visual amenity   The value of a particular area or view in terms of what is seen.

Visual effect   Change in the appearance of the landscape as a result of development. This can be positive (i.e. beneficial or an improvement) or negative (i.e. adverse or a detraction).

Visual envelope   Extent of potential visibility to or from a specific area or feature.

Visualisation   Computer simulation, photomontage or other technique to illustrate the appearance of a development.

Worst-case situation   Principle applied where the environmental effects may vary, for example, seasonally to ensure the most severe potential effect is assessed.

Zone of visual influence   Area within which a proposed development may have an influence or effect on visual amenity.

References

[1] Council of the European Communities (1995) *Directive on the assessment of the effects of certain public and private projects on the environment*, 85/337/EEC.

[2] Commission of the European Communities (1997) Directive 97/11/EC Amending Directive 85/337/EEC.

[3] Town and Country Planning, England and Wales (1999) *Town and Country Planning (Environmental Impact Assessment) Regulations 1999*, HMSO.

[4] Swanwick, C., Department of Landscape, University of Sheffield and Land Use Consultants (forthcoming) *Landscape Character Assessment: Guidance for England and Scotland*, Countryside Agency/Scottish Natural Heritage.

[5] Department of Environment (1995) *Preparation of Environmental Statements for Planning Projects that Require Environmental Assessment: A Good Practice Guide*, HMSO.

[6] Department of Environment, Transport and the Regions, Planning Policy Guidance Notes, *PPG 15 Planning and the Historic Environment*.

[7] *The Bruntland Report on our Common Future* (1987) HMSO. See also, DoE (1990) *This Common Inheritance*, HMSO.

[8] Department of Environment, Transport and the Regions, Planning Policy Guidance Notes, *PPG 1 General Policy and Principles*.

[9] Land Use Consultants (1991) *Landscape Assessment Planning Principles and Practice*, Countryside Commission for Scotland (SNH).

[10] Scottish Natural Heritage (1996) *Assessing The Natural Heritage Resource: A Guidance Note for Local Authorities*, Scottish Natural Heritage.

[11] Welsh Office Circular 1999 *Environmental Impact Assessment (Assu'r Amgylchedd)*, bilingual publication.

[12] Countryside Commission (1997) CCX 44 1997, *The Character Map of England*, Countryside Commission/English Nature.

[13] *Natural Heritage Zones: Planning: The Wise Use of Scotland's Natural Diversity* (2000) Scottish Natural Heritage Publications.

[14] Price, G. (1995) *Landscape Assessment for Indicative Forest Strategies*, Forestry Authority.

[15] Countryside Council for Wales (1998) *LANDMAP: The Landscape Assessment and Decision Making Process: Handbook for Consultants*, Countryside Council for Wales.

[16] Department of Transport/Scottish Office Industry Department/The Welsh Office/Department of the Environment for Northern Ireland (June 1993) *'Environmental Assessment', the Design Manual for Roads and Bridges* Volume 11, The Welsh Office.

Further reading

Bond, A. (2000) *Environmental Impact Assessment in the UK*, Chadwick House.

CAG Consultants and Land Use Consultants (1997) *What Matters and Why: Environmental Capital: A New Approach – A Provisional Guide* (report prepared for the Countryside Commission, English Heritage, English Nature and Environment Agency).

Commission of the European Communities (1997) Directive 97/11/EC Amending Directive 85/337/EEC.

Department of Environment Circular 3/95 (Welsh Office 12/95) *Permitted Development and Environmental Assessment*.

Department of Environment Circular 13/95 (Welsh Office 39/95).

Department of Environment's Environment and Heritage Service (1999) *Northern Ireland Countryside Survey*.

Department of Environment for Northern Ireland, Development Control Advice Note 10 *Environmental Impact Assessment*.

Department of Transport, Scottish Office Industry Department, Welsh Office and Department of the Environment for Northern Ireland (1993) *Environmental Assessment, the Design Manual for Roads and Bridges*.

DETR (1998) *Policy Appraisal and the Environment*, HMSO.

DETR (1999) *Environmental Impact Assessment*, Circular 02199, HMSO.

DETR (2000) *Guidance on the Methodology for Multi-Modal Studies*.

EC DG XI Environment, Nuclear Safety and Civil Protection May 1999 (Hyder) *Guidelines for the Cumulative Impacts as well as Impact Interactions*.

Glasson, J., Therivel, R., Chadwick, A. (1994–99) *Introduction to Environmental Impact Assessment*, UCL Press.

National Assembly for Wales and DETR (Department of Environment, Transport and the Regions) (November 2000) *Environmental Impact Assessment: A Guide to Procedures*, HMSO.

Petts, J. (ed.) (1999) *Handbook of Environmental Impact Assessment Volume 1*, Blackwell Science.

The Scottish Executive Development Department Planning (September 1999) Advice Note Pan 58 *Environmental Impact Assessment*.

Scottish Natural Heritage (1996) *Assessing the Natural Heritage Resource: A Guidance Note for Local Authorities*, Scottish Natural Heritage Publications.

Scottish Office Environment Department Circular 26/94 (1994) *The Environmental Assessment (Scotland) Amendment Regulations 1994*.

124

Swanwick, C. Department of Landscape, University of Sheffield and Land Use Consultants (forthcoming) *Landscape Character Assessment: Guidance for England and Scotland*, Countryside Agency/Scottish Natural Heritage.

Town and Country Planning, England and Wales (1999) *Town and Country Planning (Environmental Impact Assessment) Regulations 1999*, HMSO.

Appendices

Planning guidance and sources

Useful web sites

Countryside Agency and Scottish Natural Heritage; Landscape Character Assessment Guidance for England and Scotland
http://www.countryside.gov.uk/cci/guidance

Department of Environment Planning Service
http://www.doeni.gov.uk/planning

Department of Environment, Transport and the Regions (DETR); Environment Assessment Guidance
http://www.planning.detr.gov.uk/eia/assess/doc12htm

Department of Environment, Transport and the Regions (DETR); Planning Policy Guidance Notes
http://www.planning.detr.gov.uk/ppg/index.htm

Department of Environment's Environment and Heritage Service
http://www.ehsni.gov.uk

Scottish Development Department (SDD); Planning Policy Guidance
http://www.scotland.gov.uk/library3/planning/nppg/tpsr-oo.asp

Appendix 2

The legislative framework to EIA

Useful web sites

Department of Environment, Transport and the Regions Environmental Assessment page
http:/gdetr.gov.uk/eia/assess/index.htm
and
http://www.hmso.gov.uk/legis.htm

EIA Centre, Manchester University
http://www.art.man.ac.ukZeia/eiac.htm

EIA Unit of the European Commission
http://europa.eu.int/comm/dg11/eia/home.htm

IEMA, Lincoln and Edinburgh, UK
http://www.iema.net/

Oxford Brookes University Impacts Assessment Unit
http://www.brookes.ac.uk/schools/planning /research/iau.html

Penelope Project, Imperial College, London (UK EIA legislation and case studies)
http://www-penelope.th.ic.ac.uk/

The IEMA review grades and criteria for review of EIAs

Institute of Environmental Management and Assessment: EIA review grades

A Excellent, no tasks left incomplete

B Good, only minor omissions and inadequacies

C Satisfactory despite omissions and inadequacies

D Parts well attempted, but must, as a whole be considered just unsatisfactory because of omissions and/or inadequacies

E Poor, significant omissions or inadequacies

F Very poor, important tasks poorly done or not attempted

N/A Not applicable. The review topic is not applicable or relevant in the context of this statement.

Institute review criteria

Description of the development, the local environment and the baseline conditions

Description of the development

The purpose and objectives of the development should be explained. The description of the development should include the physical characteristics, scale and design, as well as quantities of material needed during construction and operation. The operating experience of the operator and the process, and examples of appropriate existing construction plant, should also be given.

Site description

The area of land affected by the development should be clearly shown on a map and the different land uses of this area clearly demarcated. The affected site should be defined broadly enough to include any potential effects occurring away from the construction site (for example, dispersal of pollutants, traffic, changes in channel capacity of watercourses as a result of increased surface run off, etc.).

Residuals

The types and quantities of waste matter, energy and residual materials and the rate at which these will be produced should be estimated. The methods used to make these estimations should be clearly described, and the proposed methods of treatment for the waste and residual materials should be identified. Waste should be quantified wherever possible.

Baseline conditions

A description of the environment as it is currently and as it could be expected to develop if the project were not to proceed. Some baseline data can be gathered from existing data sources, but some will need gathering and the methods used to obtain the information should be clearly identified. Baseline data should be gathered in such a way that the importance of the particular area to be affected can be placed into the context of the region or surroundings and that the effect of the proposed changes can be predicted.

Identification and evaluation of key impacts

Identification of impacts and method statement

The methodology used to define the project specification should be clearly outlined, in a method statement. This statement should include details of consultation for the preparation of the scoping report, discussion with expert bodies (for example, planning authority, Environment Agency, English Nature, Countryside Commission or Scottish Natural Heritage, etc.) and the public, and reference to panels of experts, guidelines, checklists, matrices, previous best practice examples of Environmental Assessments on similar projects (whichever are appropriate). Consideration should be given to impacts that may be positive or negative, cumulative, short or long term, permanent or temporary, direct or indirect. The logic used to identify the key impacts for investigation and for the rejection of others should be clearly explained. The impacts of the development on people, flora and fauna, soil, water, air, climate, landscape, material assets, cultural heritage or their interaction should be considered. The method statement should also describe the relationship between the promoters, the planning, engineering and design teams and those responsible for the ES.

Prediction of impact magnitude

The size of each impact should be determined as the predicted deviation from the baseline conditions, during the construction phase and during normal operating conditions and in the event of an accident when the proposed development involves materials that could be harmful to the environment (including people). The information and data used to estimate the magnitude of the main impacts should be clearly described and any gaps in the required data identified. The methods used to predict impact magnitude should be described and should be appropriate to the size and importance of the projected disturbance. Estimates of impacts should be recorded in measurable quantities with ranges and/or confidence limits as appropriate. Where necessary, qualitative descriptions should be as fully defined as possible (for example, 'insignificant means not perceptible from more than 100m distance').

Assessment of impact significance

The significance of all those impacts that remain after mitigation should be assessed using the appropriate national and international quality standards where available. Where no such standards exist, the assumptions and value systems used to assess significance should be justified and the existence of opposing or contrary opinions acknowledged.

Alternatives and mitigation

Alternatives

Alternative sites should have been considered where these are practicable and available to be developed. The main environmental advantages and disadvantages of these should be discussed in outline, and the reasons for the final choice given. Where available, alternative processes, designs and operating conditions should have been considered at an early stage of project planning and the environmental implications of these outlined.

Mitigation

All significant adverse impacts should be considered for mitigation and specific mitigation measures put forward where practicable. Mitigation methods considered should include modification of the project, compensation and the provision of alternative facilities as well as pollution control. It should be clear to what extent the mitigation methods will be effective. Where the effectiveness is uncertain or depends on assumptions about operating procedures, climatic conditions, etc., data should be introduced to justify the acceptance of these assumptions.

Commitment to mitigation

Clear details of when and how the mitigation measures will be carried out should be given. When uncertainty over impact magnitude and/or effectiveness of mitigation over time exists, monitoring programmes should be proposed to enable subsequent adjustment of mitigation measures as necessary.

Communication of results

Presentation

The report should be laid out clearly with the minimum amount of technical terms. An index, glossary and full references should be given and the information presented so as to be comprehensible to the non-specialist.

Balance

The environmental statement should be an independent objective assessment of environmental impacts not a best case statement for the development. Negative impacts should be given equal prominence with positive impacts, and adverse impacts should not be disguised by euphemisms or platitudes. Prominence and emphasis should be given to predict large negative or positive impacts.

Non-technical summary

There should be a non-technical summary outlining the main conclusions and how they were reached. The summary should be comprehensive, containing at least a brief description of the project and the environment, an account of the main mitigating measures to be undertaken by the developer, and a description of any remaining or residual impacts. A brief explanation of the methods by which these data were obtained and an indication of the confidence which can be placed in them should also be included.

Appendix 4

Strategic Environmental Assessment (SEA)

The proposed Strategic Environmental Assessment Directive (COM(99)73), which is currently in consultation, is seen as the second phase in the process begun in 1985 with the adoption of the EIA Directive for projects. The European Commission has amended the proposed SEA Directive to address a limitation inherent in project EIA, namely that a number of important policy decisions will have been taken before the project level is reached which then limit the room for manoeuvre at the detailed project level (EC, 1999).

SEA is one of the tools by which sustainable development and use of resources can be most effectively implemented. Simple steps toward sustainability such as efficient energy use, multi-modal transport design and specific land-use policies can be appraised and re-structured through SEA to ensure that planning policies, plans and programmes are sustainable and hence that the projects that fall under these will be equally sustainable. This is known as 'tiering'. The figure overleaf shows the hierarchy of decision-making processes that may take place within the planning system. Effective SEA at early stages in the 'tiering' will result in shorter, better focused and more cost-effective assessment at lower levels.

Advantages of SEA

SEA therefore presents many advantages for the effective strategic consideration of environmental issues including:

- SEA encourages the **consideration of environmental objectives** during policy, plan and programme activities within non-environmental organisations.

- Facilitates **consultations** between authorities on, and enhances public involvement in, evaluation of environmental aspects of policy, plan and programme formulation.

- May remove the need for project-EIA for certain activities if their impacts have been anticipated and assessed adequately at the strategic level.

- Allows formulation of standard or **generic mitigation measures** for later projects.

- Encourages **consideration of alternatives** ignored or not feasible in project-EIA.

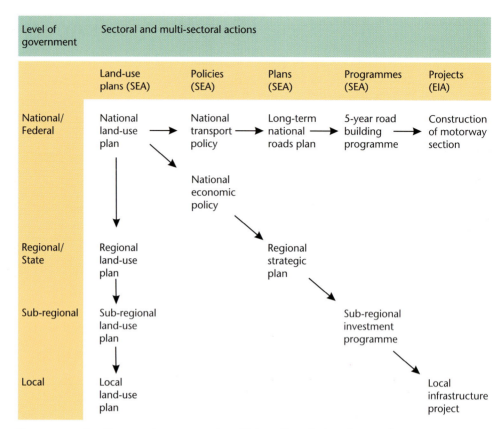

Sequence of actions and assessments within a tiered planning and assessment system

Source: *Sectoral and Multi-sectoral Actions* (EIA Centre, 1995).

Note
(...) category of action and type of assessment.

- Can help determine appropriate sites for projects subsequently subject to EIA.

- Allows more effective **analysis of cumulative effects** of large and small projects.

- Encourages and facilitates the consideration of **synergistic effects**.

- Allows more effective consideration of ancillary or secondary effects and activities.

- Facilitates consideration of **long range and delayed impacts** and impacts that are felt at the **global scale** (for example, greenhouse gases).

- Allows analysis of the **impacts of policy**, which may not be implemented through projects.

These attributes of SEA contribute to its value as an instrument in promoting sustainable development. However, there are some technical and procedural limitations to SEA.

Technical limitations

The collection and analysis of relevant baseline data for assessment purposes at the strategic level is often extensive and time-consuming. The spatial limits are less well defined, the number of alternative options are greater and the impacts are often more diverse. The level of uncertainty (i.e. confidence in the data) is usually greater with SEA due to the large number of variables affecting the future after the policy, plan or programme has been implemented due to economic, social and environmental changes that may not be feasibly predicted during the SEA process. Any SEA represents a snapshot of the current state of the environment and knowledge available at that time.

Procedural limitations

Unlike project-EIA, SEA does not have a definitive end point where the proposal achieves consent or rejection. Like EIA, SEA is an iterative process, with the outcomes of the assessment being fed back into the design stage. However, SEA is more complex with the outcomes of impact evaluation being continually recycled and the Planning Policy Programme (PPP) reviewed until the impact is mitigated or minimised. Ideally, SEA should be carried out at the earliest possible stage and be undertaken in parallel to the development of the PPP, rather than as an 'add-on' process at the end.

Tasks and methods

The stages of the SEA process are often prescribed by legislation, or as in the case of the UK, by official guidance and studies of best practice.

- **Screening:** to decide if SEA is necessary, using prescriptive lists, thresholds or criteria. Consultations between relevant authorities and consultees and the public may also be helpful to determine whether the PPP has environmental significance.

- **Description of the action and the environment:** the baseline condition of the environment under consideration is described as accurately as possible using standard data retrieval and monitoring, GIS, previous studies and consultations.

- **Scoping the action and the individual characteristics of the environment** against the characteristics of the proposed action in order to identify potential environmental impacts. This task may require a preliminary

Environmental Assessment, checklists, matrices, simulations, case studies or expert opinion.

- **Impact prediction:** the magnitude of the environmental impact is calculated using computer modelling, population and economic forecasting and cause–effect analysis.

- **Impact evaluation** to assess the significance of the impact magnitude predicted using objective evaluation methods, for example, a comparison with environmental standards or cost–benefit analysis.

- **Mitigation measures** to be identified to prevent, minimise, reduce or reverse the significant environmental impacts noted in the process.

- **Evaluation of alternatives:** the viable alternative options should then be compared and evaluated using a cost–benefit analysis, goals achievement matrices, scoring and weighting systems or the application of evaluation criteria.

- **Report preparation:** the report should present the results of the SEA process in a form suitable for evaluation by the public and other interested bodies.

- **Review:** evaluation or review of the report using consultation, in-house or external review checklists or comparison to official guidance or legislation.

- **Consultation and participation** should feature throughout the SEA process from the earliest possible stages through public meetings, exhibitions and distribution of questionnaires.

- **Decision making:** the results of the SES should enable the 'competent authority' to determine the modifications that may be necessary to the action prior to implementation.

- **Monitoring and post-auditing** to ensure that the SEA process was accurate and can assist in measuring any 'uncertainties' previously identified during scoping and prediction.

Appendix 5

Sources of useful information in the UK

Ancient Monuments Society
British Astronomical Society
The British Horse Society
CADW (Historic Wales)
The Civic Trust
The Council for British Archaeology
Council for the Protection of Rural England
Countryside Agency
Countryside Council for Wales
Department for Environment, Food and Rural Affairs
English Heritage
English Nature
Environment Agency
Forestry Commission
The Garden History Society
The Georgian Group
Historic Scotland
Local Planning Authorities
Local Tourist Offices
Meteorological Office
National Park Authorities
National Trust
Northern Ireland Environment Service
Northern Ireland Heritage Service
The Ramblers Association
Regional Development Agencies
Regional Tourist Boards
The Royal Fine Arts Commission
Scottish Natural Heritage
SMR's held by County Councils
Society for the Protection of Ancient Buildings
The Victorian Society
Wildlife Trusts

Appendix 6

Examples of threshold criteria used by practitioners

Example 1   Based on criteria of Terence O'Rourke plc

Definition of magnitude/Degrees of effects on visual amenity

The following is based on six classifications of the degree of impact.

None   No part of the development, or work or activity associated with it, is discernible.

Negligible   Only a very small part of the proposals is discernible and/or they are at such a distance that they are scarcely appreciated. Consequently they have very little effect on the scene.

Slight   The proposals constitute only a minor component of the wider view, which might be missed by the casual observer or receptor. Awareness of the proposals would not have a marked effect on the overall quality of the scene.

Moderate   The proposals may form a visible and recognisable new element within the overall scene and may be readily noticed by the observer or receptor.

Substantial   The proposals form a significant and immediately apparent part of the scene that affects and changes its overall character.

Severe   The proposals become the dominant feature of the scene to which other elements become subordinate and they significantly affect and change its character.

It should be noted that these definitions can apply to either existing or proposed situations and that impacts need not necessarily be detrimental. For example, a proposed prominent group of trees might have a 'substantial' impact, but the effect on the landscape and views would be beneficial.

Example 2   WynThomasGordonLewis

Extracts from Proof of Evidence of Mary O'Connor, DipLA, MSc, MLI, November 1997.

Public Inquiry for the extension of an existing opencast coal site, 500m south of the boundary of Brecon Beacons National Park. Reasons for refusal: detrimental effects on the landscape and enjoyment of the National Park. Main sources of impact: clearance operations; the excavation, overburden mounds; haul roads/vehicles; workshops, coal stocking, water treatment areas and lighting.

Criteria applied to the assessment of visual impact

Distance   The greater the distance, the less detail is observable and the more difficult it is to distinguish the site from its background, diminishing potential impact.

Elevation   When a viewpoint is lower than the site feature, it is more likely to be viewed against the sky, increasing its impact. When the viewpoint is higher than the site, it is viewed against a backdrop, diminishing the impact.

Size   The greater the proportion of the view occupied by the features and activities, the greater the impact. Colour and form can increase or diminish impact, by drawing the eye or by providing camouflage.

Context   The degree to which the development is in character with the context, whether urban or rural; features in the view such as landform or vegetation which frame, mask, filter, highlight, etc., the view of the site.

Weather conditions   Clarity of the air and the angle and direction of the sun at different times of year affect visibility. Upland areas are more prone to misty, cloudy and rainy conditions, reducing visibility. Haze is frequently present, especially in views towards the coast even in fine weather conditions.

Activity   Movement of vehicles and light reflection changing with movement, draw the eye, increasing impact. Static, neutral-coloured, sympathetic form diminishes adverse impact.

Change   The degree of change in the view and the rapidity of the process of change affect the degree of impact.

Criteria applied to significance and sensitivity

The **significance** of impacts, whether adverse or beneficial, was graded by relating the degree of change to the **sensitivity** of the feature or view. **Sensitivity** was related to the importance of a landscape feature within the site, or of the landscape of the site within its wider context. **Indicators** of significance and sensitivity included protective designations, areas of nature or heritage conservation interest, scenic quality or the presence of detracting features.

The criteria for grading impact significance were summarised as follows:

- Where a **sensitive** viewpoint or feature is subject to great or moderate change, then the impact is described as **significant**.

- Where the change is moderate and the view or feature is **moderately sensitive**, then the impact is described as **moderate**.

- Where the change is small, and the view or feature is of **low or moderate sensitivity**, then the impact is described as **slight**.

- In landscape terms, the ability of the extension site to accommodate change was assessed as **good** with potential for enhancement, and the sensitivity of the landscape as **low** to **moderate**.

Example 3   Nicholas Pearson Associates

Criteria taken from scoping report.

Visual impacts

Visual impacts on properties, rights of way, roads and recreational areas within the Visual Envelope, are assessed against the representative viewpoint analysis, and changes to the view are factually described. These are then assessed against the defined significance criteria based on the Highways Agency guidance set out in the DMRB volume 11.

Significance criteria for visual impact

Substantial adverse impact   Where the scheme would cause a significant deterioration in the existing view.
Moderate adverse impact   Where the scheme would cause a noticeable deterioration in the existing view.
Slight adverse impact   Where the scheme would cause a barely perceptible deterioration in the existing view.
Slight beneficial impact   Where the scheme would cause a barely perceptible improvement in the existing view.
Moderate beneficial impact   Where the scheme would cause a noticeable improvement in the existing view.
Substantial beneficial impact   Where the scheme would cause a significant improvement in the existing view.
No change   No discernable deterioration or improvement in the existing view.

Significance criteria for landscape effects

A textual ranking is given depending on the extent to which the proposals improve, cause damage, or are neutral with respect to landscape features.

Significance	Definition
Severe adverse	The proposed scheme would result in effects that
	are at a complete variance with the landform, scale and pattern of the landscape;
	would permanently degrade, diminish or destroy the integrity of valued characteristic features, elements and/or their setting;
	would cause a very high quality landscape to be permanently changed and its quality diminished.

Major adverse	The proposed scheme would result in effects that
	cannot be fully mitigated and may cumulatively amount to a severe adverse effect;
	are at a considerable variance to the landscape degrading the integrity of the landscape;
	will be substantially damaging to a high quality landscape.
Moderate adverse	The proposed scheme would
	be out of scale with the landscape or at odds with the local pattern and landform;
	will leave an adverse impact on a landscape of recognised quality.
Minor adverse	The proposed scheme would
	not quite fit into the landform and scale of the landscape;
	affect an area of recognised landscape character.
Neutral	The proposed scheme would
	complement the scale, landform and pattern of the landscape;
	maintain existing landscape quality.
Minor beneficial	The proposed scheme has the potential to
	improve the landscape quality and character;
	fit in with the scale, landform and pattern of the landscape;
	enable the restoration of valued characteristic features partially lost through other land uses.
Moderate beneficial	The proposed scheme would have the potential to
	fit very well with the landscape character;
	improve the quality of the landscape through removal of damage caused by existing land uses.

Example 4   Jeff Stevenson Associates

Determination of quality – Alternative 1

The approach adopted for landscape assessment is normally based upon the methodology developed by the Countryside Agency where consideration is given to both the objective and the subjective or aesthetic factors associated with the landscape before a judgement can be given. In this way there is a balance between landscape character and individual landscape features and elements. This could result in a process of categorisation as follows

Exceptional/Very good   Areas that exhibit a strong positive character with valued features that combine to give the experience of unity, richness and harmony. These are landscapes that may be considered to be of particular importance to conserve and which may be sensitive or very sensitive to change.

Good/Medium   Areas that exhibit positive character but which may have evidence of degradation/erosion of some features. Change may be unlikely to be detrimental.

Poor/Very poor   Areas generally negative in character with few, if any, valued features. Scope for positive enhancement.

Determination of quality – Alternative 2

Concerning landscape quality, the following definitions might also be considered

High   Areas that exhibit a very strong positive character with valued features that combine to give an experience of unity, richness and harmony. These are landscapes that may be considered to be of particular importance to conserve and which may be particularly sensitive to change in general and which may be detrimental if change is inappropriately dealt with. 'Exceptional' may be used to describe smaller areas of especially high quality or landscapes which, by virtue of the geographical extent of their positive attributes, may also be described as exceptional, for example AONB's, National Parks.

Medium   Areas that exhibit positive character but which may have evidence of alteration to/degradation/erosion of features resulting in areas of more mixed character. Potentially sensitive to change in general; again change may be detrimental if inappropriately dealt with but it may not require special or particular attention to detail.

Low (Poor/Very poor)   Areas generally negative in character with few, if any, valued features. Scope for positive enhancement frequently occurs.

The table below has been assembled from various proofs of evidence supplied to public inquiries. Criteria to determine categories of landscape quality are not exhaustive and final classification should take account of the location and relative condition of adjacent areas. The applicability of these criteria is based on the subjective judgement of the landscape professional who may also consider scenic value, completeness, scale, unity, harmony and visual amenity.

Category	Criteria	Typical example
High – exceptional	Strong landscape structure, characteristics, pattens, balanced combination of landform and landcover;	Internationally or Nationally recognised e.g. all or great majority of World Heritage Site, National Park, AONB
	Appropriate management for land use and landcover;	
	Distinct features worthy of conservation;	
	Sense of place;	
	No detracting features.	

High	Strong landscape structure, characteristic patterns and balanced combination of landform and landcover;	Nationally, Regionally recognised e.g. parts of National Park, AONB, all or great majority of AGLV
	Appropriate management for land use and landcover but potentially scope to improve;	
	Distinct features worthy of conservation;	
	Sense of place;	
	Occasional detracting features.	
Good	Recognisable landscape structure, characteristic patterns and combinations of landform and landcover are still evident;	Nationally, Regionally recognised e.g. localised areas within National Park, AONB, AGLV. Locally recognised e.g. all or great majority of Area of Local Landscape Importance.
	Scope to improve management for land use and land cover;	
	Some features worthy of conservation;	
	Sense of place;	
	Some detracting features.	
Ordinary	Distinguishable landscape structure, characteristic patterns of landform and landcover often masked by land use;	
	Scope to improve management of vegetation;	
	Some features worthy of conservation;	
	Some detracting features.	
Poor	Weak landscape structure, characteristic patterns of landform and landcover are often masked by land use;	
	Mixed land use evident;	
	Lack of management and intervention has resulted in degradation;	
	Frequent detracting features.	
Very poor	Degraded landscape structure, characterisitic patterns and combinations of landform and landcover are masked by land use;	
	Mixed land use dominates;	
	Lack of management/intervention has resulted in degradation;	
	Extensive detracting features.	
Damaged landscape	Damaged landscape structure;	
	Single land use dominates;	
	Disturbed or derelict land requires treatment;	
	Detracting features dominate.	

Source: Bradshaw, A.D. and Chadwick, M.J. *The Restoration of Land.*

Note
Derelict means 'land so damaged by industrial or other development that it is incapable of beneficial use without treatment'.

Determination of value

The following is based on the DETR's *Guidance on the Methodology for Multi-Modal Studies* and subsequently modified/extended.

Value		Typical criteria	Typical scale	Typical examples
High	Exceptional	High Importance (or Quality) and Rarity. No or limited potential for substitution.	International, National	World Heritage Site, National Park, AONB
	High	High Importance (or Quality) and Rarity. Limited potential for substitution.	National, Regional, Local	National Park, AONB, AGLV, LCI, ALLI
Medium	Medium	Medium Importance (or Quality) and Rarity. Limited potential for substitution.	Regional, Local	Undesignated but value perhaps expressed through non-official publications or demonstrable use.
Low	Poor	Low Importance (or Quality) and Rarity	Local	Areas identified as having some redeeming feature or features and possibly identified for improvement.
	Very poor	Low Importance (or Quality) and Rarity	Local	Areas identified for recovery.

The above could overcome the potential problem of an area being of limited value in a broad context but highly valued by local minority. An area of Low Importance or Quality and Rarity at a district-wide scale might well be regarded as of High Importance and Rarity (possibly irreplaceable) at the local or micro scale. What is required is the exercise of professional common sense, discretion and judgement on the part of the assessor in recognising the potential duality of response.

Determination of magnitude   Option 1

The following is based on the DETR's *Guidance on the Methodology for Multi-Modal Studies* modified/extended.

Magnitude	Typical criteria
Major	Loss of attribute(s); effect on integrity in terms of coherence, structure and function across an area sufficient to destroy the ability to retain/sustain the elements that give it its raison d'etre.
Moderate	Effect on attribute(s); effect on integrity in terms of coherence, structure and function across an area sufficient to erode or undermine the ability to retain/sustain the elements that give it its raison d'etre.
Minor	Effect on attribute(s); effect on integrity in terms of coherence, structure and function across an area sufficient to reduce the ability to retain/sustain the elements that give it its raison d'etre.
Negligible	None of the above apply.

One of the problems with the above is that it implies all change to be adverse, or, if not expressly adverse, unwelcome. The alternative below suggests a form of words that seeks to be neutral thus avoiding any implicit judgement as to the acceptability or otherwise of change.

Determination of magnitude   Option 2

Magnitude	Typical criteria
High	Total loss of or major alteration to key elements/features/characteristics of the baseline i.e. pre-development landscape or view and/or introduction of elements considered to be totally uncharacteristic when set within the attributes of the receiving landscape.
Medium	Partial loss of or alteration to one or more key elements/features/characteristics of the baseline i.e. pre-development landscape or view and/or introduction of elements that may be prominent but may not necessarily be considered to be substantially uncharacteristic when set within the attributes of the receiving landscape.
Low	Minor loss of or alteration to one or more key elements/features/characteristics of the baseline i.e. pre-development landscape or view and/or introduction of elements that may not be uncharacteristic when set within the attributes of the receiving landscape.
Negligible	Very minor loss or alteration to one or more key elements/features/characteristics of the baseline i.e. pre-development landscape or view and/or introduction of elements that are not uncharacteristic with the surrounding landscape – approximating the 'no change' situation.

Example 5   David Jarvis Associates

PREDICTED VISUAL IMPACTS WITH MITIGATION

NATURE OF IMPACT

Viewpoint Ref:	Location	Description	Level of importance					Duration (years)	Predicted impact			Nature of impact				Magnitude	Receptor sensitivity	Significance
			I	N	R	D	L		A	N	B	ST	LT	R	IR			
		View of established woodland, landscape frontage and filtered views of buildings.						—								VH	M	High
S5	Footpath L91 (east)	Limited view of construction of upper warehouse and office units at 0.5–1.2km distance in the context of an urbanised poor quality view.						2								M	ML	Medium
		Limited view of part of the completed construction uppermost elevations and within site.						15								M	ML	Medium
		Views of established woodland.														H	ML	Med–High
RESIDENTIAL PROPERTIES																		
S6	Hemington House	Restricted and filtered views of construction of warehouse and office units at 0.15km distance over 3.0m high screen bund and reinforced hedge planting in the context of a poor quality view containing significant urban elements.															H	Med–High
		Restricted and filtered views of upper levels of the side elevations of two completed warehouse units above establishing reinforced hedge planting and woodland planting.						5									H	Med–High
		Filtered views of established woodland planting above established hedgerow.															H	Med–High
S7	Property Netherfield Lane	Filtered views of construction of warehouse and office units at 0.3km distant behind grassed and planted 3m high screen bund and reinforced hedge planting in the context of a poor quality view containing significant urban elements.														H	H	Med–High

KEY

Predicted impact   A = Adverse; N = Neutral; B = Beneficial

Nature of impact   ST = Short term; LT = Long Term; R = Reversible; IR = Irreversible

Magnitude and sensitivity   N = Negligible; VL = Very Low; L = Low; ML = Medium–Low; M = Medium; MH = Medium–High; H = High; VH = Very High

LANDSCAPE IMPACTS

Topic area	Description of impact	Magnitude	Sensitivity	Level of importance					Impact			Nature				Significance
				I	N	R	D	L	A	N	B	ST	LT	R	IR	
DISTRICT LEVEL																
	Change in landscape features, characteristics or qualities															Not significant
LOCAL/PARISH LEVEL																
Landform	Scale/context of landform change	N	L						▨				▨			Not significant
Landuse	Scale/context of landuse change	M	L						▨				▨			Medium–Low
Landcover	Scale/content of landcover change	M	L						▨				▨			Medium–Low
Landscape character	Overall effects	M	L						▨			▨				Medium–Low
Landscape quality	Overall short term effects	M	L						▨			▨				Medium–Low
	Overall long term effects	M	L								▨					Medium–Low
SITE ITSELF																
Landform	Scale/context of landform change	VL	L						▨				▨			Not significant
Landuse	Scale/context of landuse change	VH	L						▨	▨			▨			Medium–High
Landcover	Scale/context of landcover change	VH	L						▨	▨			▨			Medium–High
Features	Loss of hedging	ML	L						▨			▨				Medium–Low
	Loss of woodland/scrub	ML	L						▨			▨				Medium–Low
	Loss of agricultural land	MH	L								▨					Medium–High
	Gain of hedging	VH	L								▨					Medium–High
	Gain of trees/woodland	VH	L										▨			Medium–High

KEY

Magnitude and sensitivity   N = Negligible; VL = Very Low; L = Low; ML = Medium–Low; M = Medium; MH = Medium–High; H = High; VH = Very High

Level of importance   I = International; N = National; R = Regional; D = District; L = Local

Impact   A = Adverse; N = Neutral; B = Beneficial

Nature   ST = Short term; LT = Long Term; R = Reversible; IR = Irreversible

Appendix 7

Guidelines on computer-based techniques for landscape and visual impact assessment

Visibility mapping

The visual envelope map

A visual envelope map (VEM) outlines the area of land within which there is a view of any part of the proposed development. Therefore all changes in visual impact must occur within these areas. The production of VEMs requires some skill and experience and it is recommended that they are prepared either by a landscape architect or in liaison with one.

Where smaller developments are being considered this may be constrained by intervening landscape features such as fences, hedges, woodland and buildings, topography etc. Where larger developments are being considered the range of visual influence may be determined by distance from the site.

By determining the visual envelope it is possible to identify the potential extent of visibility and potential views which could be affected. It should be appreciated that VEMs are not accurate indicators of the level of significance of the impact in the view, but merely a statement of the fact of intervisibility.

Visibility mapping can be used throughout an assessment process. It is useful as an appraisal technique at the early stages of site design and assessment to determine the potential visibility of a site compared to a similar development located on an alternative site. It can also be used for the consideration of concept layout and design alternatives to establish the potential visibility of different options. At a detailed assessment stage it can be used to identify the visibility of a specific aspect or aspects of the development.

Although the VEM is used as a working tool for the designer in his or her assessment of the visual effects of alternative designs it can also be of use in presenting the results of studies. Where the potential visual envelope extends for several miles and beyond the point at which the development would be perceptible to the human eye, the VEM should clearly state the limits of visibility. The basic assumption for the preparation of VEMs is that the observer eye height is 1.8m above ground level.

In analysis of road schemes it is important to remember that visual intrusion is occasioned by traffic on the road as well as by the road itself. A height 4m above the carriageway should be taken to represent the top of the average commercial vehicle. Lighting effects are measured at lantern height. This data needs to be used in generating the 3D model of the scheme.

To prepare a VEM it is necessary to have level data for the surrounding area of the scheme under study. This can be based on either an Ordnance Survey data or aerial photography. OS Profile data (available at scale 1:10,000) however, gives no indication of the height of buildings or trees. Where aerial surveys have been carried out they are likely to be plotted to a 1:2,500 scale with contours at two-metre intervals and provide a more accurate representation of the scene than do the OS maps at a less detailed scale. VEMs are difficult to produce directly from maps for urban areas since comprehensive information about building heights is not readily available. More extensive site inspection will then be necessary. The accuracy of a computer calculated ZVI or VEM is dependent upon the level of detail of the data that is used for the calculation process. The VEM should be checked periodically to see that account has been taken of any changes in tree cover or the presence of buildings that have occurred since its preparation.

Once a terrain model is completed, the computer can be used to generate ZVIs and cross sections very quickly. These can be used to verify the visibility of part of a development or the intervisibility of different schemes, such as wind farms. Sections can also be included in this way as part of the illustration material.

Zone of visual influence

This can be carried out quickly and quite accurately using a combination of Digital Ground Modelling (DGM) software and Computer Aided Design (CAD) software. It must be remembered that the output is as accurate as the data used (see Data Input). Zone of visual influence (ZVI) or Visual Envelopes of any development can be refined by inputting elements such as buildings in the terrain model of an area. In both cases, on-site checks are needed to ensure that the final ZVI or VEM is as accurate as possible. ZVIs can be developed from cross sections but this is considerably more laborious.

Data input

OS Digital Data may be obtained in a variety of formats at different scales for inputting topographical information into a computer. Landline data based on 1:1250, 1:2500 and 1:10,000 scales is available. This information does not include topographical information. Landform information is available at 1:50,000 scale and is supplied in 20km tiles. This information is suitable for most visual impact assessment projects with 10m contour intervals. 5m contour intervals are better for flatter sites and these sheets can be ordered from the OS at 1:10,000. It may be necessary, for accuracy, to survey and digitise additional data, such as spot heights (i.e. peaks and valleys) and additional contours in the vicinity of the site from more detailed maps. An OS Digital Licence is required to hold data, and copyright permission is required from OS to digitise additional data. It is important to note that any changes to purchased OS data should always be explained and clarified, as they may either increase accuracy or introduce human error. Note all OS information comes with specified tolerances for example ± 1500mm.

Stereoscopic height data from aerial surveys is very useful, particularly where access may be restricted for conventional surveying or to obtain heights of reference points, such as transmission towers or chimneys. Several specialist companies provide such a service at different scales and can provide a disc with the required data. It is important to base any assessment or new images on the most up-to-date photographs and verify information on site. It is also essential to state the degree of accuracy obtained, for example ±300mm.

It is most useful to plot out ZVIs as overlays over OS maps at an appropriate scale. This enables the potential visibility of different options to be compared, allows the study area to be refined and potential viewpoints to be identified. ZVIs can also be generated to show where part of a development may be visible from. This refinement can indicate, for example, where the whole structure such as a wind turbine, or just the blades, may be visible or the permeability of a structure, such as a stack or pylon. If an existing structure such as a transmission line is being replaced or upgraded, a ZVI should first be produced for the existing structure as part of the base-line information, to allow a comparison to be made.

The final presentation output is most useful if plotted on an original OS base map. A composite ZVI may be used, for example, in a wind farm combining individual ZVIs for each wind turbine. In such a case, it must be made clear that the visual envelope indicates areas where all or part of the development may be seen. Some software programmes can provide visibility maps that indicate the numbers of structures such as transmission towers or wind turbines, i.e. 1–10, or 10–20, which may be visible. It is also important to remember that a ZVI is a theoretical model and that since its provenance lies purely with contour data, the screening effect of above ground site features such as plantations or buildings has not been allowed for.

Computer presentation techniques

Introduction

During the 1990s, the quality of presentation techniques and technical drawing, in particular computer aided drafting, advanced significantly. Driven by a geometric growth in computing power, the software industry closely matched the improved potential of desktop computing with an array of sophisticated graphics packages. The raising of public awareness of computer graphics has led to a growing expectation that all professionals with a strong visual dimension to their work should keep abreast of these advances.

While expectations may be raised, there remains a challenge and responsibility to make a discerning use of technology – in some instances mixing traditional techniques with the new – to ensure that accurately communicating an issue determines the choice of graphic technique. The following notes suggest a framework for identifying an appropriate technique with a client, followed by a selection of computer graphics applications which can be tailored to make presentations more informative and cost effective.

Spatial Information Systems

Spatial Information Systems (SIS) and Geographical Information Systems (GIS) are especially useful in Environmental Impact Assessment and in particular in an integrated approach to landscape and visual assessment on large scale projects. SIS and GIS provide powerful tools whereby layers of data on a variety of topics can be collated, sieved, selected or superimposed. This can be particularly useful in collating and comparing baseline data which may include vegetation cover and habitat distribution, topography, soils, archaeological sites, population and settlement data, drainage catchments, transportation, land use, cultural features and landscape character areas.

Potential alternative developments and their possible sources of adverse effects can similarly be tested in relation to potential receptors and baseline data. SIS and GIS systems work well in the production of base maps, but can also incorporate three-dimensional modelling to create terrain models, intervisibility zones and fly through imaging.

Illustrative techniques

Each method for creating a variety of presentation techniques is considered below. The precise choice of technique for a particular scheme will depend on the data available, timing and budget. Several economies may also be identified, for example using the same CAD model to generate an accurate two-dimensional perspective which may then in turn form the basis of a three-dimensional animated sequence.

Two-dimensional techniques

Photomontages

Until recently, photomontages were most commonly prepared by manually painting the details of a development (often in oils or gouache) onto a photograph and then re-photographing the finished product for use in reports or as display boards. The more common approach today is to scan the photograph or panorama of photographs into the computer and, using a graphics package, eliminate the junctions between each photograph by selecting, copying and pasting areas of coloured points (pixels) from adjacent photographs over the join until it is obscured. This is more easily achieved if adjacent photographs are spliced in areas with less detail.

Once a seamless base photograph is available to show the 'before' image, details of the 'after' proposed image can be created on a separate layer in the graphics package. Technically accurate details of the proposal are usually imported from CAD software, which should offer an ability to set a camera position to view the proposal from the same location as the original photograph was taken. When the perspective has been accurately determined the proposed structure is transferred to the graphics package and rendered to produce a realistic interpretation of the proposed development.

With time and skill, a variety of filters and effects such as light and shadow may be employed to reveal a product that may be hard to distinguish as a photomontage from an 'as-built' photograph. For additional realism, additional foreground information layers may also be added, placing trees, shrubs, people and vehicles in the foreground of the montage.

Photomontages may be commissioned for a variety of purposes, for example as marketing images conveying a general impression of a proposal (where they should be described as for illustrative purposes) or as technically accurate photomontages designed to conform to the rigour of planning applications and public inquiries. The latter require painstaking attention to accuracy and detail. However as both products may appear graphically similar it is vital that all parties understand the distinction between each, the associated costs and time to prepare and the end use to which they will be applied. Before starting work it is also essential to establish the largest size output print that will be needed. Larger prints mean larger file sizes, which can be reduced if high quality outputs are not required. Modern printers can achieve clear outputs at almost any size subject to the image being prepared originally to a sufficiently high resolution.

Three-dimensional animation

Often there is a need to portray complex developments in more detail than can be easily achieved using a single or several photomontages. An example may be where there is a requirement to select a large number of viewpoints, moving perhaps from an aerial to a ground perspective and on into the interior of a building. An animated sequence may also be helpful in explaining the orientation of a site more dynamically than a series of single photographs can achieve.

In exactly the same way as a traditional physical model can vary in its level of detailing, three-dimensional computer models can also range from simple massing studies to inclusion of significant levels of detail such as incorporating scanned images of site signage. Inevitably, attaining a high level of detail takes considerable time and raises costs, hence the importance of clarifying the purpose of the model before assessing an appropriate level of detail with the client.

A three-dimensional animation usually starts by importing two-dimensional OS or site survey data to establish the footprint of a proposal and the surrounding context. The third dimension of the height of existing buildings may be determined by triangulation, and the height of a proposed structure taken from the architects' or engineers' plans, preferably in CAD format. After the basic massing model is complete, static views from a series of angles are generated and a 'preview route' or 'path' around the model is agreed with the client before the process of rendering each individual frame is commenced. A three minute animation will require around 2,700 individual frames to be rendered, the speed of which will depend on the computer's ability to handle multiple calculations of perspective and lighting effects. Changes to the original agreed route through the model at this stage are time consuming and expensive, often requiring a complete re-rendering of the model.

Frequently the photo-realism of animated three-dimensional models encourages their use in documents, reports and publicity material. Since any single rendered frame within a three-dimensional model may be output as a two-dimensional image, producing a perspective is a fairly straightforward task. With both the two-dimensional and three-dimensional output, additional information can be added as text in subtitles or as interleaved frames, and for the three-dimensional animation a voice-over may offer additional explanation of the project.

Perspectives and full animation may also be cost-effectively duplicated for distribution on a CD-ROM.

Interactive virtual reality models

Photomontages though relatively inexpensive suffer the limitation of requiring early selection of a fixed viewpoint(s) and offer no ability to change the nature of the proposal without starting again. Animation sequences follow predetermined paths, and take considerable time to amend and re-render the chosen route if changes are required. And these course corrections can be frequent in genuine planning negotiation and public consultation. Clients anticipating a need to respond rapidly to such changes may find the benefits of virtual reality (VR) come to the fore. No less important is the ability to respond to a neighbour affected by development who asks reasonably 'How will the view from my house change as a result of this proposal?'. Here again, short of preparing a photomontage for each and every viewpoint, VR can play an important role.

A virtual reality model is a three-dimensional computer model, which permits the viewer to 'fly', 'walk', or 'drive' through a representation of a development proposal. Within the bounds of the area modelled – often known as the VR world – the onlooker can select any route and stop at will to examine views in any direction. The VR model can also be set up with options to turn various development proposals on or off. Typically this may include adding or removing buildings, changing the number of storeys, altering a flat to a pitched roof, or altering the colour or texture of cladding materials until it satisfactorily respects the building line prescribed by neighbouring properties.

Each of the above options is often said to be viewed in real time, yet in some respects the VR model can also offer interactivity in the fourth dimension. Illustrating change over time is frequently important in predicting the degree to which planting may screen a development in the future. Based on growth tables for a known planting mix, the benefit of a tree belt may be shown at say five, ten, and fifteen years' growth, while still offering the facility to move freely around the site. This degree of flexibility is a powerful tool for objectively predicting and then mitigating impacts before major changes to site layout prove necessary.

The manner of creating a VR model for planning and Environmental Assessment work is largely as described above for massing out a three-dimensional animation. Perhaps the main subsequent difference between three-dimensional animation and VR is that in the latter technology the time consuming process of rendering surfaces with textures is cut down in order that movement around the model remains fluid.

Progress in the development of VR software also means that this is now available on both PC and Macintosh platforms. Most business applications are viewed on an ordinary monitor or in public consultation on a screen utilising a digital projector. Navigation around a model is achieved using a standard mouse and keyboard options.

Other techniques

Other visualisation techniques which are generally less quantitative and credible may be appropriate under certain circumstances. The possibilities include overlays and perspective sketches – often constructed over computer-generated wire lines. Physical models tend to be expensive, but are very useful in public consultation. By contrast, photographs of similar developments are generally inexpensive and can be remarkably helpful, provided it is made clear that they are indicative only. Artist's impressions, which are not accurately constructed, should be avoided.

Summary

Depending on budget, time-scale and the complexity of the proposal for which visual impacts are to be considered, each of the above methods has its strengths. Irrespective of the chosen technology, the objective – encouraged by open government and Local Agenda 21 initiatives – is to move toward a process of planning by consent. Of all the procedures discussed, virtual reality appears to be offering most promise in this area enabling the client, planners and the public to comment on and influence proposals at an early stage. Importantly the technology also permits schemes to be relatively easily adapted and modified to take account of a spectrum of opinion and professional judgement.

Appendix 9

Guidelines on photomontage and CAD

A photomontage is the superimposition of an image onto a photograph for the purpose of creating a realistic representation of proposed or potential changes to a view. Traditionally these were created manually by hand rendering, but today most are generated *using computer imagery*. Photomontages are prepared as follows:

Field photograph of development site taken from fixed viewpoint

35mm film format with a 50mm lens is recommended for most developments. If a practitioner wishes to use an alternative focal length, then a 50mm photograph of the same view should be provided for comparison. The practitioner should also explain the reasons for his choice of format and lens.

All details of the format of the photograph and the focal length should be noted and be consistent between different views of the same proposal unless otherwise stated.

The viewpoint must be fixed, either at a known Ordnance Datum, i.e. at a benchmark, due to tolerances in Ordnance Survey data or by surveying the camera position to provide a precise co-ordinate. The angle of direction through the centre of the lens should also be recorded, with the height of the camera above ground level.

The location and height of at least three reference points in the photographic view will need to be recorded or surveyed. These might include a visible building or transmission tower, or a known triangulation point, height of landform or landmark.

Panoramas

Where a wider field of view than can be achieved from a single photograph is required, a series of overlapping photographs is taken from the same viewpoint, again using the recommended 35mm film format with a 50mm focal length for the lens. There should be a 50 per cent overlap between adjacent photographs. The photographs are then scanned into a computer and 'joined together' using a graphics package; minor 'retouching' to eliminate slight variations in colour tone between photographs is acceptable. This is more easily achieved if adjacent photographs are spliced in areas with little detail.

Preparation of geometric perspective based on available information for proposals

The degree of detail in the montage will very much depend upon that available in the proposals. For all development, basic dimensions of buildings, structures or landform will be required, as will information of colour, finishes and landscape design elements. Examples of brickwork, plant material etc. can be scanned into the computer to provide a library of finished textures.

Technically accurate details of the proposal are usually imported from CAD software offering an ability to set a camera position to view the proposal from the same location as that of the original photograph. When the perspective has been accurately determined the proposed structure is transferred to the graphics package and rendered up to produce a realistic interpretation of the building.

Superimposition of perspective image onto a base photograph and rendering (black and white or colour) of that image to produce the photomontage

High-quality computer-generated montages, where the perspective has been accurately set up, are of considerable value in presentation. The use of the computer technique of photomontage allows ready incorporation of future image modifications and can rapidly be revised as the scheme is 'firmed up'. They can also later be used to test the visual impact of alternative layouts and development form and grouping.

Printing a photomontage to provide copy (prints or slides)

Before starting work it is essential to establish the largest size output print that will be needed. Larger prints mean larger file sizes, which otherwise may be reduced if high quality outputs are not required. Modern printers can achieve clear outputs at almost poster size subject to the image being scanned originally at a sufficiently high resolution. It is important to ensure that before and after photographs are reproduced using the same printer settings to achieve direct comparison of the images.

Summary

Photomontages may be commissioned for a variety of purposes. As images conveying a general impression of a proposal they must be clearly annotated 'for illustrative purposes'. As technically accurate photomontages designed to conform to the rigour of planning applications and public inquiries they require painstaking attention to accuracy and detail. Both products may appear graphically similar and it is therefore vital that all parties understand the distinction between each, the associated costs and time to prepare, and the end use to which they will be applied.

Appendix 10

Checklist for landscape and visual impact assessment

Desk studies

current and historical OS and other maps
aerial photographs
geology, soils maps, hydrology survey
land cover and land use maps
development plans/planning policies
landscape designations – statutory and non-statutory
survey and issue reports, other planning documents
countryside strategies, landscape assessments/guidelines
archaeology, ecology, buildings, settlements
other conservation interests/historic and cultural associations
common land and rights of way
meteorlogical office data
topographical analysis, geological and drainage features
patterns and scale of landform, land cover and built development, landscape
    character
potential receptors of effects
    – important landscape components
    – settlements
    – valued landscapes
    – residents, other groups of viewers
    – visitors or travellers through the area

Field survey (structured survey form)

extent of visibility
localised screening effects
viewpoints within study area with photos
identify sensitive receptors
woodland, tree and hedgerow cover
landcover (or vegetation apart from trees) and land use
field boundaries and artefacts
archaeological, historic and cultural features
access and rights of way
seasonal screening effects

Consultations

agencies, for example, Scottish Natural Heritage, Countryside Commission for Wales, Countryside Agency, English Heritage, Highways Agency, Environment Agency, Cadw
local planning/regulatory authority
local amenity, conservation bodies, for example, Archaeological Trust, DEFRA, Royal Society for the Protection of Birds

Analysis

scale and character
physical and human influences
current trends for change
destructive elements, features
spatial organisation
character areas
– reflecting scenic, visual, archaeological
historical, ecological, built environment, cultural associations
quality (condition)
value and importance
landscape designations
– reasons, rarity, national/regional context
scenic quality
– context
– importance of components
– condition of important components including management and deviation from optimum
conservation interests or features
cultural associations
– writings, paintings
perceptions of local value
sensitivity
– tolerance of change/constraints upon development
change or enhancement potential
– conservation, restoration, creation of new features, planning gain
visual analysis
– visibility from surrounding areas
– elements interrupting, filtering, influencing views
– principal viewpoints
– annotated photos

Report structure

Landscape setting
site location, land use, settlement,
topography, drainage, vegetation
landscape context and character

Planning policies
landscape designations, TPOs
rights of way, long-distance paths
other amenity or nature conservation value

Site features
topography, drainage
land use, vegetation, settlement
features of ecological, cultural or archaeological interest
access, rights of way, level of use
views
major service routes

Landscape character (character areas)
location, character type
features and views contributing to its character, significance
landscape quality/importance

Receptors and sensitivity, ability to accommodate change
settlement
vegetation, land use
site features
landscape character
views
public paths, access

Opportunities and constraints

Sources of impact

potential construction impacts
potential operational impacts
removal of existing features, landform, vegetation
introduction of new features, landform, vegetation
change in landscape character
changes in views
magnitude of change
duration of the impact, change in effects over time

Index